HOLY LIVING

HOLY LIVING
Saints and Saintliness in Judaism

LOUIS JACOBS

JASON ARONSON INC.
Northvale, New Jersey
London

10 9 8 7 6 5 4 3 2 1

Library of Congress Cataloging-in-Publication Data

Jacobs, Louis.
Holy living : saints and saintliness in Judaism / Louis Jacobs.
p. cm.
Includes bibliographical references.
ISBN 0-87668-822-9
1. Jewish way of life–History of doctrines. 2. Perfection–Religious aspects–Judaism–History of doctrines. 3. Jewish saints–History of doctrines. 4. Judaism–Doctrines. I. Title.
BM723.J28 1989
296.6'1–dc20 89-39274
CIP

Manufactured in the United States of America. Jason Aronson Inc. offers books and cassettes. For information and catalog write to Jason Aronson Inc., 230 Livingston Street, Northvale, New Jersey 07647.

For David and Maya

CONTENTS

PREFACE

Throughout the history of Judaism there can be discerned that specific quality of extraordinary piety known as *Hasidut,* roughly corresponding to the term *saintliness.* The person whose life is permeated with this quality is known as a *hasid.* This book is a phenomenological study of *Hasidut* and the *hasid,* that is, it seeks to delineate the special characteristics of saintliness in Judaism, showing how these differ from other types of Jewish religious belief and conduct. It is somewhat odd that, while the subject has received attention in general works on Judaism, there has not been, to my knowledge, any detailed examination of the phenomenon of saintliness as a separate subject of study.

While this book provides a popular account for which prior knowledge on the part of the reader is not necessary, it is hoped that scholars of Judaism, and of religion in general, will find some stimulus for further research into this fascinating topic.

Chapter 1 examines the concept of saintliness as it appears in the Bible and talmudic literature and through medieval Jewish thought and life down to the present day. The common features are described, as are the different manifestations in Jewish history.

Learning and piety are not only at variance in religious life but are frequently in conflict. The tensions between learning and saintliness, between the ideal of the *hakham* (*sage*) and the *hasid,* are noted in Chapter 2.

Chapter 3 deals with such questions as: How does a person proceed in order to become a *hasid?* What does training for the saintly life consist of? Which are the techniques to be used? Is it desirable to have saintly ambitions?

The saint is ruthless in the demands he makes on himself. As a spiritual extremist, he abhors spiritual apathy, compromise, or indulgence. The history of religion demonstrates clearly the imbalance of the saintly life. A certain lack of proportion is the price the saint is willing to pay in his quest for the Divine. This aspect of saintly extravagance is treated in Chapter 4.

The saintly attitude of equanimity in Jewish sources, going back to the time of the Stoics, is examined in Chapter 5. Typical of the saintly ideal is the attitude of complete indifference to both the praise and the opprobrium of human beings. To be concerned with what other people think of him is, for the saint, a severe hindrance to his burning need to be alone with his God.

The joy and rapture experienced by the saint is the intense, though unsought, reward for his spiritual strivings. A description of saintly rapture is presented in Chapter 6.

Patterns of saintly behavior are studied in Chapter 7. Throughout the ages and in every religion, the saint has been expected to follow a severe regimen of pious conduct, possible only for those in the closest communion with the transcendent.

Although actual evidence, as opposed to pious legend, is scanty, the belief persists that the saint possesses supernatural powers. In the canonization process of the Catholic Church, miracles have to be adduced in evidence before a man or woman can be declared a saint. While there are no such official processes in Judaism, this does not mean there is a denial that the holy man is capable of overriding nature. Chapter 8 describes the many claims in the hagiographical literature of Judaism in which saints possessed supernatural powers.

The elevated stage that the saint attains at the time of his death is the subject of Chapter 9. The descriptions of this awesome moment owe much to standard beliefs as to what happens when the saint's soul departs this life.

Finally, Chapter 10 discusses the veneration of saints, a highly sensitive topic in Judaism, where worship is due to God alone. A constant battle has been fought against superstitions that border on idolatry.

ACKNOWLEDGMENTS

It would not have been possible to embark on this enterprise without the help provided by the massive research of a host of scholars, Jewish and non-Jewish, whose works are referred to in the text and footnotes. My indebtedness to them is great. My thanks are due to the editors at Jason Aronson Inc. for their high standards of production, and especially to Arthur Kurzweil for his unfailing help and encouragement. As always, I am grateful to my wife Shula for putting up with my very unsaintly moods when I am writing a book . . . and not only then.

1

JEWISH SAINTLINESS THROUGH THE AGES

Every religion has, in addition to its ordinary adherents, men and women whose lives are dedicated to heroic virtue and who display extraordinary, self-denying religious commitment–for example, the Christian *saint,* the Muslim *wali,* the Hindu *guru,* the Buddhist *bodhisattva.* With a borrowing of terms from one religion to another, these religious types are referred to in English by various names: saints, gurus, holy men, hermits, anchorites, miracle workers, and so forth. They are sometimes found in groups or fraternities, bound together by a common aim, but sometimes distinguished as individual pietists, operating on their own both within and apart from the general social order. This book examines the phenomenon of saintliness as it appears in the history of Judaism.[1]

The usual term for the phenomenon of saintliness in Judaism is *Hasidut,* an abstract noun used to describe the kind of life embraced by the *hasid,* a term that must be examined because of the way it is used in the Bible and the rabbinic literature.[2] I am indebted to Gulkovitsch's monographs, but his treatment of this term in the Bible deals mainly with the concept as it appears in the Psalms,[3] and his study of the rabbinic material examines only those stories concerning "a certain *hasid.*"[4] So it remains to trace in greater detail the evolution of the term from the Bible through rabbinic and talmudic literature.

HESED

The term *hesed,* found in numerous passages in the Bible, denotes mercy, loving kindness, loyalty, fidelity, grace, or charm, according to the context in which it occurs. However, in two passages–"And if a man shall take his sister . . . it is *hesed,*" (Leviticus 20:7) and "Righteousness exalteth a nation but sin is *hesed* to any people" (Proverbs 14:34)–the word appears to mean "shame" or "reproach." (It is possible, however, that the conventional meaning is intended in Proverbs, so that the latter verse should be translated, "but *hesed* is sinful to a people," that is, excessive generosity is out of place in *national* affairs.[5]) The word occasionally has this meaning of "reproach" in Aramaic, and scholars have remarked on the idea of "eager zeal" and "intensity" as basic to the root of the word.[6] It is almost as if the ancient writers had in mind the very quality of superabundance, which finds its normal expression in the good but which at times produces the opposite by bursting its bonds.

The practice of *hesed* is a frequently occurring theme in the biblical books. The prophet Micah (6:8) speaks of God relinquishing His anger because He delights in *hesed.* In the books of Joel (2:13) and Jonah (4:2), God is described as "abundant in *hesed.*" The same description is applied to God in the book of Exodus (34:6). Jeremiah speaks of God's *hesed* to His people (31:2) as well as Israel's *hesed* to God (2:2). *Hesed* is the keynote of the book of Hosea. The central theme is that God loves Israel, whom He has betrothed as His bride in *hesed* (2:21); therefore, He desires *hesed* more than sacrifices (6:6). Because of His love for Israel, God desires to be worshipped by those who practice *hesed*–that is, by those who reciprocate God's love and whose regard for others is such that every kind of social injustice and iniquity is abhorrent to them (Hosea 10:12–13; 12:7–8). *Hesed* in Hosea refers to God's condescension to human needs, to Israel's affection for God, and to people in their relationship to one another.[7] *Hesed* is a kind of spontaneous generation of good will in the human character which makes us delight in giving freely and joyously to others. It has often been noted, on the other hand, that the translation of *hesed* as "mercy" is inadequate. The word possesses no overtones of condescension, nothing patronizing or suggestive of affability to inferiors–not, at least, when the concern is with the behavior or attitudes of one person toward another. This effervescence of goodness in the character sometimes results in what we call charm. In the book of Esther, the heroine is nowhere described as a beauty. It was her charm–her *hesed*–that captivated her royal lover (Esther 2:17). R. Joshua b. Korha comments in the Talmud (*Megillah* 13a), somewhat ungallantly, that Esther was sallow, but that a thread of *hesed* was drawn about her. Schechter's interpretation of *hasidim* as people with "beautiful souls," is analogous to the verse in Esther, homiletical, and very far fetched.[8]

HASID

We turn now to the word *hasid,* derived from *hesed.* It must be noted that, unlike the English word *saint,* from the Latin *sanctus,* the term *hasid* in its original biblical usage has no overtones of consecration or dedication to a special life of extreme holiness and piety. The biblical *hasid* is certainly no charismatic personality, but simply one who practices *hesed,* one whose heart and mind are suffused with a rich intensity of goodness resulting in complete devotion to God and unqualified love of others. God Himself is described in the Book of Psalms (114:17) as *hasid.* To speak of the Creator as "good" is understandable; to speak of him as "saintly" is merely grotesque.[9]

There are references in the Bible to the "man of *hesed*" (Proverbs 11:17; Isaiah 57:1), and the term *ish hesed* may be a synonym for *hasid.* But it is probable that *hasid* is the more intensive of the terms, as in the distinction between "So-and-so swims" and "So-and-so is a swimmer."

The feminine form of *hasid* is not found in the Bible. The form *hasidah* is used to describe a certain bird in Leviticus (11:19), Deuteronomy (14:16), Jeremiah (8:7), Zechariah (5:9), Psalms (104:17), and Job (39:13). In all of these passages (with the exception of the verse in Job, where the rendering is "ostrich"), the Authorized Version (AV) translates the word as "stork." The word may have no connection with *hasid* and may not even be a Hebrew word. In the Talmud (*Hullin* 63a), R. Huna explains the word to mean "shows kindness (*Hasidut*) to its companions," but this no more than a folk etymology.[10]

In the Book of Psalms there are references to the *hasidim,* plural of *hasid* (37:28; 79:2; 89:5; 97:10). Who were these men? Is the term *hasidim* nothing more than a generic term for the righteous and godly, or does it designate a special group of men dedicated to a special purpose? It is impossible to answer this conclusively. When the psalmist, for instance, refers to God speaking peace to His people and to His saints (*hasidim,* Psalm 85:9), are the words "to His saints" in apposition to "to His people," or is it a reference to a special group of "saints" among the people? Many scholars are inclined to the view that in some of the psalms, the *hasidim* are none other than the men with this name who fought on the side of the Maccabees against Antiochus. Psalm 149 in particular speaks, apparently, of a group of battling saints. Gulkovitsch's ingenious attempt to trace the development of *hasid* and *hasidim* in the psalms from a general term for the whole community to a special cultic group within the community is not very convincing because of the difficulty, acknowledged by him, of accurately dating the various psalms.[11]

WHO WERE THE HASIDIM?

The *hasid* of the Bible is not, then, a specially consecrated individual, a man set apart from others. He is not a "type" at all, but merely an exceptionally good and pious man. It is possible, however, that in the period of the psalms, pious individuals formed themselves into groups for the defense of their faith when it was under attack. If this is correct, then these individuals–the *hasidim*–may have formed the group of that name in the time of the Maccabees; or, they may have been an earlier group out of which the later group grew. Of this we can be certain–that in the Maccabean revolt, a company of men joined the ranks of the rebels and were known as *hasidim.*

The earliest definite references to a group of dedicated men calling themselves *hasidim* are in the books of the Maccabees, where it is stated that these men (*Assidaioi* in Greek) attached themselves to the Maccabees (1 Maccabees 2:42–44; 7:8–18) and, according to another version, were the group of which Judas Maccabeus was the captain (2 Maccabees 14:3–6). Scholars long ago noted that there is internal evidence (the use of Greek words, for instance) that the Book of Daniel was composed during the Greek period. It is plausible that the book was written during the Maccabean revolt to encourage the Jews to remain steadfast in their loyalty to the faith of their fathers, though Pfeiffer's categorical statement that the book was actually composed by a *hasid* goes beyond the evidence.[12] The conjecture that the Book of Daniel was composed during the Maccabean periods finds some support in the account (7:19–22) of Daniel's vision of the "fourth beast" who made war "with the saints" (though the Aramaic word used here is *kaddishin,* "holy ones").

It is clear that there is uncertainty of identification between the *hasidim* of Psalms and the *hasidim* of the books of the Maccabees. Are the references in both books to the same group, or did the Maccabean group grow out of an earlier group–or is it possible that the term *hasidim* in Psalms is not the name of any particular group? These are questions that have no final answers. All that can be stated with certainty is that a group of men known as *hasidim* took part in the Maccabean revolt. Maccabees 1 and 2 do not, in fact, speak of a special group banding itself together in order to fight against Antiochus specifically; rather, they speak of a group already in existence. M. Burrows may be right in tracing an unorganized puritanical tendency beginning with the Rechabites (Jeremiah 35:6–7) and appearing in the *hasidim* of the later psalms–the "poor" who trust in God to deliver them. Out of this group emerged the Maccabean *hasidim.*[13]

THE ESSENES

The suggestion that the word *Essenes* is a Greek form of the word *hasidim* was made long ago,[14] but the identification is still far from certain. The Essenes lived a monastic life in which possessions were shared. They lived chiefly in the neighborhood of the Dead Sea, and there has been much conjecture about whether they are to be identified with the Qumram sect. (According to Philo, there were around 4,000 in number). When not working, they engaged in religious study and prayer. To identify positively the Essenes with the Maccabean *hasidim* or to ascribe to them the Book of Jubilees, Enoch, and other books is precarious, however, due to the paucity of evidence.[15] In any event, there is no explicit reference to the Essenes in the rabbinic literature, so later accounts of Jewish saintliness owe nothing to this group in any direct manner.

There are a number of references in the rabbinic literature to *hasidim ha-rishonim,* "the pious men of old." This group may have been the Essenes or possibly the earlier Maccabean group. Again all is conjectural, the material on these *hasidim* in the rabbinic literature dating from a much later period. We should not, therefore, read the rabbinic accounts as if they were anything like contemporary records. It is said that these *hasidim* would empty their minds one hour *before* their prayers in order to direct their minds to God (Mishnah *Berakhot* 5:1; *Berakhot* 32b); they would attach fringes to the corners of their garments (Numbers 15:37–41) as soon as three handbreadths of the garment had been woven, even though the law demanded only that the fringes be attached when the finished garment was to be worn (*Menahot* 41a); and they would consort with their wives only on Wednesdays, in the belief that a conception on any other day might result in the child being born on the Sabbath, which would involve a degree of Sabbath desecration – permitted, of course, but avoided by the *hasidim* taking the most extreme precautions (*Niddah* 38b).

The same scrupulous regard displayed by these *hasidim* in connection with religious duties was displayed by them, it is said, in connection with their social responsibilities. It was their practice to take extreme measures to prevent anything that belonged to them from doing harm to others (*Bava Kama* 30a). For example, they were known to bury their thorns and broken glass in the middle of their fields at a depth of three handbreadths. In the very late post-talmudic tractate *Semahot* (3:10), it is stated in the name of R. Judah (second century) that many of these *hasidim* died of self-induced intestinal disorders, as a result of purging themselves so that they could enter paradise in purity. The picture of the *hasidim ha-rishonim* that emerges from the rabbinic literature is of men scrupulous in ritual and social behavior far beyond the letter of the law.

The looser biblical term *hasidim* is now applied to a particular pietistic group. It is impossible to state whether there is in all this an authentic tradition reaching back to the *hasidim ha-rishonim* or, indeed, whether such a group of *hasidim* ever existed except in the minds of later teachers. Nevertheless, reference is made to the *hasidim ha-rishonim* in the later rabbinic sources, and this in itself contributed much to their being used as the model for many subsequent deliberations on the nature of the saintly ideal.

The fact that these *hasidim* are referred to as *ha-rishonim* is evidence that by the second century, when the Mishnah was compiled, the group was no longer in existence. Yet in using the term *hasidim,* the later sources demonstrate that the *hasid* was viewed as an exceedingly pious individual, outstanding in love of God and of others, and extremely scrupulous in religious observance. The *hasid* has now become virtually the equivalent of the saint.

THE HASID IN THE MISHNAH

The best way to introduce the concept of the *hasid* as it appears in the rabbinic talmudic literature is to note the references in tractate *Avot* (Ethics of the Fathers). This tractate of the Mishnah affords us a properly representative model.

The first reference to a *hasid* in this tractate is in a saying attributed to Hillel: "An ignorant man (*am ha-aretz*) cannot be a *hasid*" (2:6). In the same chapter (2:8), the names of Rabban Johanan ben Zakkai's five chief disciples are given and one of these, R. Jose the Priest, is described as a *hasid.* When the disciples were urged by their master to "go out and see" the good way a man should choose and the evil way he should shun, R. Jose returned with the advice that a man should choose to be a good neighbor and shun a bad neighbor (2:9). R. Jose's special series of maxims is "Let the property of thy fellow be as dear to thee as thine own; and fit thyself for the study of the Torah, for it is not thine by inheritance; and let all thy deeds be done for the sake of Heaven" (2:12). Here the essence of saintliness is good neighborliness in all its aspects, application to the study of the Torah, and lack of self-interest. These features pervade the history of Jewish saintliness.

An anonymous teaching in a later chapter of *Avot* describes *Hasidut* as intensely virtuous behavior. Of the four possible character types, the *hasid* is the one who says "What is mine is thine and what is thine is thine" (5:10). Of the four kinds of tempers, the *hasid* is the most difficult to provoke and the most easily pacified (5:11). Of the four types of almsgivers, the *hasid* gives of himself and wishes others to give (5:13). Of the four who frequent the House of Study, the *hasid* not only goes there but also practices what he has studied there (5:14).

The picture that emerges from the foregoing is of the *hasid* as a man who is not content with the normal standards of observance, and who resolves to go far beyond the letter of the law. This idea is found in other rabbinic sources as well. Thus the ruling is given that if a money-changer had given deficient coins, the victim can receive compensation only if he returns to make his claim during the limited period in which he is able to discover that he had been cheated; it is assumed that if he does not make the claim within this short period, he has waived his rights. But a ruling of the Mishnah is quoted in which it appears that the victim can make his claim any time during a whole year. To resolve the contradiction, R. Hisda (d. 309) suggests that the much longer period stated in the Mishnah is a rule for saints (*mishnat hasidim*) (*Bava Metzia* 52b). Similarly, if a wealthy traveler finds himself without money in a strange town, he may not only take from the poor relief funds of that town, but he is not obliged to pay back what he has taken, since "at that time he was a poor man." In another ruling, however, it is stated that he *does* have to return the money. Again R. Hisda resolves the contradiction: The ruling that he must make restitution is a rule for saints (*Hullin* 130b). Both these instances, it is worth noting, are said to be recorded in a Mishnah – that is, in an official code. Whether R. Hisda's interpretations are correct is beside the point, as is the attribution to R. Hisda. In the latter case we may have an example of the well-known device used by the editors of the Talmud of attributing to a teacher subject matter with some resemblance to his name (a pun on *Hisda* and *hasidim*).[16] It remains true that, at least in the opinion of the editors of the Talmud, there are statements in the official code that are not directed to everyone, but rather are intended only for those who wish to pursue saintly conduct. In other words, the "saintly rule" is precisely that–not a matter of individual preference, but in the nature of an actual code to which the *hasidim* are obliged to conform.

In this connection the following anecdote, told in the Jerusalem Talmud (*Terumot* 8:6, 46b), is instructive. The Mishnah rules that if a company of Jews are ordered by heathens to give up one of their number to be killed under penalty of having the entire group killed, they may not deliver the man unless the heathens have specified that he is the particular man whom they want to kill. R. Joshua b. Levi followed the Mishnah and saved the lives of the inhabitants of his town by handing over to be killed a man specified by name, whereupon Elijah, who used to visit R. Joshua, ceased to do so. When Elijah eventually resumed his visits to R. Joshua b. Levi, the latter excused his conduct by referring to the clear ruling of the Mishnah, to which Elijah replied, "Yes, but is it a *mishnat hasidim?*"

HASID OR TZADDIK

The difference, then, between the formally righteous man–the *tzaddik*–and the *hasid* is that the *tzaddik* observes the law, whereas the *hasid* goes beyond the letter of the law. R. Huna (third century) contrasted the two parts of the verse (Psalm 145:17) "The Lord is righteous (*tzaddik*) in all His ways" and "and gracious (*hasid*) in all His works." At first God treats sinners according to their just deserts, but in the end He is gracious to pardon; that is, He goes beyond the letter of the law (*Rosh ha-Shanah* 17b). There was a widespread belief in rabbinic times that the parings of fingernails could cause harm to a pregnant woman who stepped over them. Consequently, it is said (*Moed Katan* 18b) that one who throws the nail parings away is wicked, and one who buries them is a *tzaddik,* but the *hasid* burns them so as to eliminate any possibility of their causing harm. The *hasid* never retaliates when others insult him. The Midrash (Midrash Psalms to Psalm 86:2) states that when a man hears others insult him and remains silent, that man is called a *hasid.*

It must be recognized that the term *hasid* is sometimes used very loosely in the rabbinic literature to denote simply a good and pious man, a reversal to the original, biblical usage. It is in this sense that the term is used when it is said that the majority of sailors are *hasidim* (Mishnah *Kiddushin* 4:14); this obviously means not that the majority of sailors are "saints," but rather that, because of the hazardous nature of their occupation, they are pious. But apart from a few instances, the word does convey the concept of that extraordinary virtue that is the hallmark of the saint. In the examples given earlier, the emphasis is on saintliness as expressed particularly in prayer, in striving for self-perfection, and in care for the property of others. The Talmud (*Bava Kama* 30a) quotes the third-century Babylonian teacher R. Judah as saying that one who aspires to becoming a *hasid* must fulfill the laws found in the *Nezikin* section of the Mishnah, which deals with damages and which describes how to avoid causing harm to others. The fourth-century teacher Rava is quoted as advising the would-be *hasid* to fulfill the precepts contained in the ethical treatise of the Mishnah, *Avot.* A third opinion is then quoted that he must fulfill the matters dealt with in tractate *Berakhot* of the Mishnah, that is, with matters of prayer and benedictions.

THE DEVELOPMENT OF HASIDISM

The stages in the development of the term *hasid* have been noted from biblical times down through the rabbinic period. In the Bible the *hasid* is simply the good person who leads the good life in the sight of God and fellow humans, though with an intensity of virtue that singles him out from the ordinary run of even the virtuous. During the Maccabean period we find the name given to the members of a pietistic group. This may be the group referred to in the talmudic literature as the *hasidim ha-rishonim,* but the group was no longer in existence in the Tannaitic period (the first two centuries C.E.). During this and the later rabbinic period, the *hasid* was the man of special sanctity, altruism, and holiness; he was law-abiding, but noted for his desire to go beyond the letter of the law. With the addition of mystical and ascetic elements, the *hasid* in subsequent Jewish life and thought belongs to this late rabbinic type.

During the Middle Ages the talmudic literature had acquired

virtually canonical status and had become, for the followers of rabbinic Judaism, the most influential work; Jewish teachers and thinkers of every variety based their ideas on the Talmud, interpreting the talmudic passages to fit their predilections. For devotees of the saintly life, whether individual pietists or organized groups, the rabbinic teachings on *Hasidut* (this abstract term was generally used for the phenomenon in the Middle Ages) formed the basis of their theological stance, even when, in obedience to their own viewpoint, they read ideas into the Talmud far removed from its original intention. Because of their particular stance, a number of medieval masters were seen by their contemporaries and by subsequent generations as a part of the saintly tradition. Two teachers, in particular, were called *he-hasid,* "the saint": Bahya Ibn Pakudah (second half of the eleventh century)[17] and Jonah Gerondi (d. 1263).[18] Bahya's Arabic treatise, translated into Hebrew with the title *Hovot ha-Levavot* (Duties of the Heart), and Jonah Gerondi's *Shaarey Teshuvah* (Gates of Repentance) became classic moralistic works for the ordinary Jew, but were seen by those with ambitions of *Hasidut* as addressed especially to them.

The medieval heirs, as a group, to talmudic *Hasidut* were the *Hasidey Ashkenaz,* "the German saints," who flourished in Regensburg and in the towns of Speyer, Worms, and Mainz during the twelfth and thirteenth centuries.[19] The leaders of this group were Samuel he-Hasid (in the second half of the twelfth century), his son, Judah he-Hasid (d. 1217), and the latter's pupil Eleazar b. Judah of Worms (d. c. 1230). The two most important and influential works produced in this circle are the *Sefer Hasidim,* attributed to Judah he-Hasid, and the *Rokeah,* by Eleazar of Worms.[20] Judah he-Hasid's commentary to the Torah was recently published from manuscript by I. S. Lange.[21] In this commentary, the basic ideas of the *Hasidey Ashkenaz* are read into the scriptural verses.

Before we examine some of the ideas of the *Hasidey Ashkenaz* on the saintly ideal, it should be acknowledged that these saints were not organized in a fraternity, but rather were a circle of individuals residing in various towns in Germany in fairly loose association with one another.[22]

The *Hasidey Ashkenaz* flourished during the period of the Crusades, a time when many Jews gave up their lives for their religion. The martyrs were not necessarily scholars but ordinary pious folk for whom *Kiddush ha-Shem,* "Sanctification of the Name," as martyrdom is called, was far more than a theoretical demand; it was an ever-present reality.[23] This goes a long way toward explaining both the popular aspects of the *Sefer Hasidim,* including the superstitious,[24] and their emphasis on martyrdom. Zinberg rightly observes:[25]

> In that dark era of blood and terror, when even an ordinary Jew was prepared to be a "saint" and had to be prepared at every moment to sacrifice himself for his faith, the *Sefer Hasidim,* which was produced not by an individual but, in a sense, by the community, endeavored to arouse in the hearts of the people the fervor and mystical ecstasy of self-sacrifice and martyrdom.

At the same time, it is obvious that many of the prescriptions in the *Sefer Hasidim* and especially in the *Rokeah* are addressed to the saint in the usual connotation of the term–an individual of extraordinary sanctity and goodness.[26]

As in the Talmud, the social aspects of *Hasidut* are stressed among the *Hasidey Ashkenaz.*[27] In their efforts to help the poor, the saints sometimes came into conflict with the community leaders. The *Sefer Hasidim* contains a particular section, reading between the lines of which it can be seen that the saints occasionally conflicted with the community's leaders, who were content to obey the requirements of the strict law without any attempt to go beyond it.[28] The leaders could not agree to demands that would prove to be a constant drain on the charity chest. The following passages are revealing:

> If a man needs to be supported by others, if he is able to obtain support from the communities in each city he should not be advised to approach individuals since that which is given to him out of the community funds does not cause his heart pain, whereas if an individual gives to him he may suffer distress even when a small amount is taken from him and it is as if his blood is being taken from him. When Rava (*Bava Batra* 8b) compelled a man to give charity that man was wealthy, but it is not proper for a man himself to do this [i.e., to importune individuals]. Once people have decided to give to him, he should not bother them further, but beforehand he may tell them how poor he is. [No. 868]

> The community leaders noticed that a good Jew in the town offered hospitality to visitors. He was once a rich man who made guests so welcome that they would always visit him. After a time the man lost his wealth but the guests continued to come to him. The members of the town council were then obliged to say to the man: "We know that you are unable to spend so much on your guests, but since they still come to you please accept this charity money so that you can continue to supply your guests with food and drink." It is in order for the man to inform his guests that the money with which he supplies their needs is charity money so that they should not think they owe him a personal debt of gratitude. If, however, the guests do think that the money is his own, and if they knew it was charity money they would be ashamed to accept it, then it is better not to tell them the truth. Even though they will think it is his own money that he is spending on them, this is not to be compared to misrepresentation since he has not misled them; they have misled themselves. Furthermore, even if the host, a God-fearing man who has lost his money, is ashamed to admit to his guests that he is using charity money, it is no worse than the man who says to the charity overseers: "Give me charity for myself" and then gives the money he receives to the poor. Concerning such a case it is said: "Happy is he that considereth the poor" (Psalm 41:2). [No. 870]

What the community leaders had to say we are not told but can easily guess.

Far from almsgiving's being considered in any way a hindrance to the pursuit of the saintly ideal, it was of its essence. "Whoever is charitable will have the merit of seeing the face of the *Shekhinah*" [No. 880]. "It is better to be friendly with an ignorant man who is generous and whose reputation in business is good, than to be friendly with a scholar who is greedy and a miser" [No. 882]. The *hasid* must respect the feelings of others at all times. "If a man wishes to give gifts worth different amounts to three people, he should not give them when all three are present because those who receive the smaller gifts will resent it. He should give the gifts in private to each person and should beg each not to tell the others" [No. 897]. "If a man has lent someone money, he should try to avoid meeting his debtor for even if he does not say anything about the debt the debtor may be embarrassed, thinking to himself, the reason he does not mention the debt is because he suspects that I am reluctant to repay it" [No. 901].

The picture that emerges from the writings of the *Hasidey Ashkenaz* is of the saints scattered throughout the various communities and pursuing the ways of benevolence, not as members of a fraternity, but as individuals willing to help others by their sense of special vocation.

Among the saintly values stressed by the *Hasidey Ashkenaz* is that of repentance.[29] This idea, that repentance is not only for a man guilty of serious sin but is also an essential ingredient in the saintly life, involves a reversal of the older rabbinic views on *Hasidut.* For example, the Talmud (*Sukkah* 53a) states that of the people assembled in the Temple courtyard for the water-drawing ceremony, the *hasidim* among them used to say, "Happy our youth that has not disgraced our old age," while the penitents would say, "Happy our old age which has atoned for our youth," seeming to suggest that the title *hasid* was given only to one whose life had been untainted by sin since youth, not to the penitent. In the talmudic discussion on which is the greater, the perfectly righteous or the penitent (*Berakhot* 34b), the term used for the righteous is *tzaddik,* not *hasid.* The Zohar (I, 39a) similarly states that while the penitent has a higher place in the celestial halls than the righteous, the highest place of all is occupied by the *hasid.* Among the *Hasidey Ashkenaz,* on the other hand, repentance for sins ("minor" sins are treated by the saint as if they were "major") is essential to saintliness. These German saints would engage in severe mortification of the flesh as a penance for their sins, rolling naked in the snow, for instance, or smearing themselves with honey to be stung by bees. Baer[30] and others have detected here the influence of the Christian monasticism of the period.

Eleazar of Worm's *Rokeah* has no fewer than twenty-eight sections on repentance (pp. 28–36). Here Eleazar records his famous four types of repentance, influential in the history of Jewish piety:

1. *Ha-baah,* "coming"–The sinner finds the same opportunity to sin as before, but this time refrains from sinning.
2. *Ha-gader,* "the fence"–The sinner denies himself even legitimate things if they are in some way connected with his sin.
3. *Ha-mishkal,* "the balance"–The sinner balances the pleasure he obtained through the commission of the sin with the pain he voluntarily inflicts upon himself.

4. *Ha-katuv,* "Scripture"–The sinner torments himself with tortures that have some affinity with the punishment stated in Scripture for that particular sin.

Although the *Rokeah* is essentially a code of law, it opens (pp. 1–19) with a section called *Hilkhot Hasidut,* "Laws [*sic*] of saintliness."[31] Here are stated twelve "roots" of saintliness, twelve principles upon which saintly conduct is based: (1) the love of God, (2) the fear of God, (3) humility, (4) having God always in the mind, (5) the beginning of *Hasidut* as going beyond the letter of the law, refusing to lie or to take revenge, (6) delight in the study of the word of God, (7) acceptance of the words of the sages, (8) purity and abstinence, (9) cleansing from every trait of sin, (10) having a good character, (11) self-improvement, (12) holiness.

Each of these twelve principles is discussed in detail. For instance, in his discussion of the fifth principle, "the beginning of *Hasidut,*" Eleazar observes that, at first, when a man is moved to follow the path of *Hasidut,* it is as hard as death itself, since people laugh at him and put him to shame so that, metaphorically, his blood is shed; and yet, since he is a *hasid,* he bears it all in love. Once he has sincerely begun to follow the saintly way, he will never relinquish it, even when he is embarrassed by their taunts or when they offer him large sums of money if only he will be like others. The *hasid* will take the utmost care not to cause any injury to others. He will refuse to associate with scoffers or with those who waste their time in idle talk, but will associate only with those who do good deeds (pp. 10–11). On the eighth principle, "acceptance of the words of the sages," Eleazar remarks that the *hasid* will drink thirstily at the fountain of wisdom provided by the sages (pp. 13–14). He will listen to the words of the very least of the sages with as much care as to the words of the greatest of them, so that he learns from all. He will allow himself to be rebuked by the sages without complaining. In much of this the *Rokeah* quotes in his support scriptural and rabbinic passages, but what he actually does is create a regimen for the *hasid* by presenting stray and random sayings in a systematic way.

Another saintly fraternity flourished among the kabbalistic mystics in sixteenth-century Safed. The two most prominent members of this circle were Moses Cordovero (1522–1570) and Isaac Luria (1534–1572), the latter always referred to not as *he-hasid,* but as *Ari ha-Kadosh,* "The holy lion." The title *kadosh* is reserved for the martyrs and for the very greatest of the saints. Schechter and Fine have studied in detail the ideas and ideals of the Safed circle and the saintly rules drawn up for the guidance of its members.[32]

At a later date, a similar fraternity was established in Jerusalem by the Moroccan kabbalist Hayyim Ibn Attar (1686–1743). At the college of Ibn Attar, the students would pray on behalf of Diaspora Jewry.[33] Ibn Attar's significance is the result, in addition to the example provided by his saintly life, of the commentary he wrote to the Pentateuch, *Or ha-Hayyim.* This commentary became a key work for aspirants to *Hasidut.* In the later hasidic movement, for example, the work was considered essential reading for the devout *hasid.* Reports of Ibn Attar's life describe him as sitting all day in his yeshivah wearing *tallit* and *tefillin* and living a holy, ascetic life, free of worldly concerns. R. Hayyim Joseph David Azulai, the *Hida,* says of him:[34]

> I had the merit of belonging to his Yeshivah and saw with mine own eyes how great was his learning. In his dialectics he uprooted huge mountains. His holiness was wondrous in the extreme. In our generation the heart of the Rabbi was like an unfailing fountain. His wisdom can be seen from the books he wrote but that was only a tenth part of his wisdom. The breadth and sharpness of his mind was a marvel of marvels. All day there rested upon him an aura of sanctity and asceticism and tremendous were his powers.[35]

It hardly needs to be said that there is nothing in Judaism to correspond to the process of beatification and canonization in the Catholic church. No process of this kind ever existed in Jewish history. It is rather the case that, by a kind of popular consensus, a few individuals were acknowledged, because of the quality of their lives and, especially of their works, to possess that extraordinary degree of sanctity thought to entitle them to be called *hasid.* This is what happened to Bahya Ibn Pakudah and Jonah Gerondi. In the eighteenth century, the renowned Italian kabbalist Moshe Hayyim Luzzatto (1707–1746), for all his youth and despite strong opposition to his views by some prominent rabbinic figures in his native Italy, came eventually to be accepted as '*he-hasid* Luzzatto'. His book *Mesillat Yesharim* (Path of the Upright) became a significant manual of instruction for those eager to follow the saintly path.

The *Mesillat Yesharim* is based on the *Baraita* attributed in the Talmud (*Avodah Zarah* 20b) to the second-century teacher R. Phinehas b. Yair, wherein are described the stages on the road to self-perfection. The *Baraita* reads:

> Knowledge of the Torah leads to watchfulness, watchfulness to zeal, zeal to cleanness, cleanness to abstinence, abstinence to purity, purity to saintliness (*Hasidut*), saintliness to humility, humility to the fear of sin, and the fear of sin to holiness.

In his introduction, Luzzatto bemoans the fact that the striving for *Hasidut* is cultivated neither by the learned, who believe that this pursuit affords little intellectual challenge, nor by the ignorant, who imagine saintliness to consist in reciting numerous psalms and long confessions, in fasting, and in ablutions in ice and snow. Believing that saintliness is an art to be cultivated, Luzzatto proceeds to depict the ascent of the ladder as described by R. Phinehas b. Yair.

> In planning this book, which is intended as a reminder both to myself and others of the prerequisites to perfect piety, I have followed the order laid down in that *Baraita.* I shall point out the different phases and details that belong to each of these requisites, the way to fulfill each of them, the hindrances that beset them, and how to be on one's guard against these hindrances. I, or anyone else who may be interested in this book, will read it with the view of learning to fear the Lord our God, and not to be remiss in our duty to Him.

Luzzatto's other-worldly stance is evident throughout the book. In the first chapter, he writes:

> It is fundamentally necessary both for saintliness (*Hasidut*) and for the perfect worship of God to realize clearly what constitutes man's duty in the world, and what goal is worthy of his endeavors throughout all the days of his life. Our Sages have taught us that man was created only to

find delight in the Lord, and to bask in the radiance of His Presence. But the real place for such delight is the world to come, which has been created for that very purpose. The present world is only a path to that goal.

It is obvious that Luzzatto aims very high in the book. In his concluding chapter on holiness (*kedushah*), Luzzatto states that one who follows the stages of this guide will merit the cleaving of his soul to the holiness of God, and it will rise to ever-greater heights until it is endowed with the holy spirit, its power exceeding human limitations.[36]

He, therefore, who cleaves to God in complete self-surrender is able to derive from Him even the power over life itself, the power which, more than any other, is the attribute of God. Thus the *Baraita* which we quoted at the beginning of the book concludes with the words: "Holiness leads to the gift of the holy spirit, and the gift of the holy spirit leads to the power of quickening the dead."

Actually, the reference in the *Baraita* to "quickening the dead" is to the Resurrection, at the end of time, but Luzzatto applies it here to the ability of the holy man to revive the dead *in this life*.

Luzzatto's *Mesillat Yesharim* influenced both the hasidic movement of the eighteenth century and the school of the anti-hasidic Elijah, Gaon of Vilna (1720–1790), "the last great theologian of classical rabbinism," as he is called by Ginzberg.[37] The Gaon is said to have declared that, had Luzzatto still been alive, the Gaon would have journeyed over land and sea to sit at his feet in order to learn how to be God-fearing. Although the Gaon's fame rests chiefly on his mastery of every branch of Jewish learning and his many works on Talmud, Codes, Kabbalah, and biblical exegesis, he, too, was called *ha-Gaon he-hasid mi-Vilna*.[38] Learning, or profound study, especially of the Talmud and the Codes, was essential for the *Hasidut* of the Gaon and his disciples. Saints in this school, regardless of the other virtues they possessed, had to express their religious yearnings in the hard discipline of Torah study by day and by night. This was the type of piety encouraged in the famed Yeshivah of Volozhyn, founded by R.

Hayyim of Volozhyn, chief disciple of the Gaon. R. Israel Lipkin of Salant (1810–1883), also known as *he-hasid,* founded the Musar movement.[39] This elitist movement, after a struggle, managed to win over to its side the majority of the Lithuanian yeshivot, all of which followed in the footsteps of the Gaon of Vilna and his disciples. The Musar teachers, who sought to develop techniques for self-improvement, devised the particular Lithuanian–Vilna Gaon type of *Hasidut,* which involved the exercise of the mind in total dedication to the study of the Torah together with the cultivation of wholesome character traits. The emphasis was on introspection and severe self-scrutiny, all accompanied by melancholy tunes. The opponents of the movement called attention to, among other aspects, its extremely somber mood, which, they held, was at variance with the joy that was such a prominent feature in all the traditional descriptions of the saintly life.

THE BAAL SHEM TOV

Separated from the *Hasidey Ashkenaz* by several centuries, there arose in eighteenth-century Poland and the Ukraine the new hasidic movement, the founder of which is generally held to have been Israel b. Eliezer (1698–1760), the *Baal Shem Tov,* "Master of the Good Name" (that is, of God, one who uses divine names for the purpose of healing; generally abbreviated *Besht*). There is little to connect directly Beshtian Hasidism with the *Hasidey Ashkenaz,*[40] but there are affinities, nonetheless, between the two groups. In reality, as scholarly research has shown, there were a number of groups at the time in that part of the Jewish world calling themselves *hasidim,* each having a charismatic leader. But these groups either vanished entirely from the scene or became assimilated into the group led by the *Besht.* The two chief disciples of the *Besht* were Jacob Joseph of Pulonnoye (d. 1782), the first author in the new hasidic vein, and Dov Baer, the Maggid of Mesirech (d. 1772), the real organizer of the movement. Eventually, the disciples of the Maggid became hasidic masters in their own right; some of them became founders of hasidic "dynasties," in which the sons and grandsons continued the tradition of the particular master. As a result, the term *hasid* could no longer be used to denote the saintly leader of the group. The *hasid* was now a "follower" of the master, and a new term, the *zaddik* (the usual spelling in English of *tzaddik*), was adopted for the master, producing, in fact, a reversal of the two roles. As we have seen, in the earlier sources the *tzaddik* was generally simply a good and righteous man, while the *hasid* was the superior "saint." Now the *hasid* is a follower of the saintly *zaddik*. Another name for the zaddik, used early on in the movement, was *rebbe,* to distinguish this new type of leader from the *rav,* the traditional rabbi, the expert in Jewish law.

A vast body of literature was produced by the hasidic movement, much of it containing guidance for saintly living, but it is often far from clear whether these teachings were intended only for the *zaddik* or for the general run of the *hasidim.* Certainly, it is frequently implied that only the *zaddik* is capable of reaching the higher stages of the saintly life. It might be noted that a similar development took place among the followers of the Lithuanian Musar movement, with the gurulike Musar personality becoming the leader of the group. In the later Musar literature this leader, too, is often referred to as *ha-Rav ha-Tzaddik,* obviously under the influence of the hasidic movement, even though the Musarists belonged within the ranks of the opponents of Hasidism from the school of the Gaon of Vilna, the *mitnaggedim.* R. Israel Salanter is reported to have said that both the *hasidim* and the *mitnaggedim* are in error–the former because they think they have a rebbe, and the latter because they think they do not need one.

THE HUNGARIAN SCHOOL

In the Hungarian school of R. Moshe Sofer (1762–1839), a form of *Hasidut* developed, different in many respects from both that of the Lithuanian-mitnaggedic and the Beshtian hasidic types. R. Moshe Sofer (the *Hatam Sofer*), Rabbi of Pressburg, a fierce opponent of the new Reform movement, was an outstanding halakhic authority and a gifted polemicist and communal leader.[41] Yet from the many glimpses we obtain of his personal life, it is clear that he can be firmly placed in the *Hasidut* tradition. His contemporary, R. Mordecai Baneth of Nikolsburg, once described him as "a living *Hovot ha-Levavot*" (the title of

Bahya's famous book).[42] His particular brand of Hungarian *Hasidut* was manifest in his descendants, successive rabbis of the Pressburg community, and in his numerous disciples of the Hungarian school.

R. Moshe Sofer's teacher during his youth in Frankfurt-am-Main was R. Nathan Adler ha-Kohen (1741–1800), known significantly as "the *hasid* among the priests" (*he-hasid she-bi-kehunah*). Adler and his disciples blended the traditional scholarly values with the characteristics of the saint.[43] Adler, influenced by R. Hayyim Modai of Jerusalem, who had been his houseguest for several years, established a private *minyan* in his home, in which he used the kabbalistic prayerbook of Isaac Luria. His departure from tradition in this and in other respects brought about conflict between Adler and the official Frankfurt community leaders. A ban was placed on Adler as a result of the conflict, so he left Frankfurt for a time. He later returned, however, to found a yeshivah, the students of which were called *hasidim.*

It is of interest that the communal rabbi of Frankfurt at the time was Phinehas Horowitz, who, in his youth, had come under the influence of the Maggid of Mesirech, the hasidic leader. As rabbi of the strongly antihasidic community of Frankfurt, however, Horowitz was bound to distance himself from any innovations of the kind introduced by Adler. A no doubt highly biased polemic against Adler's *hasidim* describes their "offenses."[44] They are excessively strict in their observance of the dietary laws; they wear two pairs of *tefillin;* their womenfolk wear *tzitzit;* they are so meticulous in observing the rite of circumcision that their infants often fall into a faint because the procedure is so lengthy. They had dreams in which they foretold the future, thereby terrifying the commonfolk with their threats of disaster. Dubnow is undoubtedly correct in seeing Adler's *Hasidut* as more akin to that of the Safed Kabbalists than to that of Beshtian Hasidism.[45]

Rabbi Moshe Sofer revered his master, even though he, like Rabbi Horowitz, had become a communal rabbi in the traditional mold and never followed Adler's type of *Hasidut.* His grandson relates that at a gathering of scholars, one of them referred to Adler as "an angel of the Lord of hosts," whereupon Rabbi Moshe Sofer, who was present, exclaimed, "And what an angel!"[46] As has been stated, Sofer and those of his school held themselves somewhat aloof from Beshtian

Hasidism.[47] Nevertheless, he had great respect for the famous hasidic masters, and they, in turn, had great admiration for his immense learning and defense of Orthodoxy.

THE SEPHARDI WORLD

The veneration of saints in the Sephardi-Oriental world had its own development, influenced it would seem by the Islamic pattern. The Sephardi-Oriental Jewish saint is not usually referred to as a *hasid,* but as *ha-rav ha-kadosh,* "the holy rabbi." This type of saint is rarely the leader of a group, as is the case in Hasidism, but rather is a holy individual to whom people of diverse backgrounds turn for his blessings and prayers on their behalf. Miracle tales of the holy men are a popular feature of Sephardi-Oriental Jewries. In recent years these tales have been widely disseminated. Examples are the biographies of the Yemenites R. Mordecai Sharabi (1912–1984) and Hayyim Savaani (1898–1979),[48] the Moroccan saint Israel Abuchatzeirah,[49] and the Jerusalem saint Yosef Sholomo Dayyan.[50]

It is clear from this introductory survey that while the phenomenon of saintliness (*Hasidut*) can be detected throughout Jewish history, it assumed a variety of forms, depending upon the particular circumstances of the time and place in which the saints lived.

2

SAINTLINESS AND LEARNING

The identification of saintliness with a lack of intellectual ability or, at least, with a preference for religious emotion over intellectual thought, overlooks the fact that many of the Jewish saints were very learned men; they were not only wise in the fear of the Lord, but they saw learning itself as an expression of the fear of the Lord. For all that, there are undoubtedly tensions between the ideal of study of the Torah as the supreme religious aim in Judaism and the saintly ideal, in which the emotions play a highly significant role, one in which religious feeling tends to override the claims of the mind. Traditionally, the sage – the *hakham* – devotes himself to the mastery of the sacred texts. Basically he is a student, endeavoring to understand the subjects he studies and to make his own contribution to the learning process. The knowledge he seeks is knowledge of the Torah, in all its ramifications. The enlightenment sought by the saint, on the other hand, is the knowledge of God, and this has a strongly mystical tinge. The saint's striving is devotional in character. For the *hakham,* knowledge of the Torah is not a means to an end; it is the supreme end in itself. For the *hasid,* knowledge of the Torah, although an elevated religious value, is a means to an end, to the passionately sought attachment to God.

When the means is sometimes at variance with his higher aim, it is the former that must yield to the latter.

Scholem, in his study of the *Hasidey Ashkenaz,*[1] remarks that, for the members of this circle, to be a *hasid* was to conform to purely religious standards, entirely independent of intellectualism and learning.[2] "For while Hasidism continued to place a premium on knowledge, it was nevertheless possible to be a *hasid* without an understanding of more than, say, the text of the Bible." Scholem considers this a departure from the older rabbinic view of *Hasidut.* But while Scholem is probably right that the schism between learning and saintliness is especially pronounced among the *Hasidey Ashkenaz,* the tension is not without parallel, even in the earlier rabbinic literature.

THE IGNORANT MAY BE HASIDIM

The saying attributed to Hillel (*Avot* 2:9) that the ignorant man (*am ha-aretz*) cannot be a *hasid* means no more than that the ignorant man is far from his ideal. A parallel saying of Hillel's, in the same passage, is that a quick-tempered man cannot teach (that is, he is not an ideal teacher). The saying that "he who studies and practices is a *hasid*" (*Avot* 5:14) does not mean that one who *does not* study cannot be considered a *hasid.* The meaning is clearly that *of the four who frequent the House of Study,* the *hasid* is the one who both studies and practices.

As a matter of fact, there are references in the rabbinic literature to the ignorant *hasid:* "Even if a scholar is vengeful and bears malice like a serpent, gird him on thy loins; whereas even if an *am ha-aretz* is a *hasid,* do not dwell in his vicinity" (*Shabbat* 63a).

Obadiah Sforno quotes this latter saying in his commentary on Moses' choice of judges.[3] Moses was advised by Jethro to choose "able men, such as fear God, men of truth, hating unjust gain" (Exodus 18:21), but later (verse 25) it states, "And Moses chose able men," and there is no mention of their possessing the other qualities. Evidently, says Sforno, no doubt thinking of the tension between saintliness and learning in his own sixteenth-century Italy, Moses was unable to find a sufficient number of persons possessing all the qualities mentioned in the previous verse, so he gave priority to "able men"–that is, men of intellectual ability–even if they were deficient in saintly qualities. As Elizabeth Wordsworth says in her famous jingle:

> If all the good people were clever,
> And all clever people were good,
> The world would be nicer than ever
> We thought that it possibly could.
>
> But somehow, 'tis seldom or never
> The two hit it off as they should;
> The good are so harsh to the clever,
> The clever so rude to the good.

A further interesting example of the antagonism between the *hasid* and the scholar in rabbinic times is found in this talmudic passage (*Shabbat* 121b): "A *tanna* recited before Rabbah, son of R. Huna: 'If one kills snakes and scorpions on the Sabbath the spirit of the *hasidim* is displeased with him." ' Rabbah retorted, "As to those *hasidim,* the spirit of the Sages is displeased with *them.*"

In view of this, Abelson[4] is far off the mark when, writing on the Jewish saintly ideal, he remarks, "One possession, however, is indispensable to him–learning. The saint must be a man of learning; and only a man of learning can be a saint." Not so. In the rabbinic tradition as well as in the Jewish tradition in general, a learned person is not necessarily a saint, and a saint is not necessarily a learned person, although, of course, there have been many in whom both ideals were combined.

There are many references in the rabbinic literature to men of extreme piety, such as Honi the Circle Drawer, Hanina b. Dosa, Abba Hilkiah, and Amram Hasida, renowned for their saintliness but not for their learning and never as teachers of *Halakhah.* It is clear beyond doubt that while such men were held in high esteem, the scholar was held to be superior to them. The distinction between the two types is penetratingly expressed in the anecdote of R. Hanina b. Dosa praying successfully for the sons of Rabban Johanan b. Zakkai, even though the great sage's prayers for his own sons had been ineffective. When the sage's wife asked, "Is Hanina greater than you?" Rabban Johanan replied, "No he is not. But I am like a prince in the presence of the king, while Hanina is like a slave in the presence of the king," by which he meant that the slave can enter the king's presence at any time to carry out his tasks, whereas the prince has to obey protocol (*Berakhot* 34b, see Rashi *ad loc.*).

In the Zohar (II, 15a) a similar anecdote is told about R. Eliezer and R. Akiba, but there the prayer of the lesser one is answered because the king wishes to keep the greater one with him for as long as possible. Moreover, in the Zoharic version, the superior man is also a man of prayer, no doubt because of the different scale of values in kabbalistic thought. It remains true that generally the scholar is not only a different type but a superior type to the man of prayer. One talmudic passage (*Bava Batra* 12a) even suggests that the sage is superior to the prophet.

The truth of the matter is that the approach of the *hasid* is bound to be in conflict with the attitudes of the official teachers of *Halakhah*. Luzzatto's attempt to reconcile the rival views can succeed only by treating saintliness itself as a kind of science requiring severe intellectual application. The antagonism between the two views flared into open warfare with the rise of Beshtian Hasidism in the eighteenth century. William James, after a careful analysis of the one-sidedness of saints, concluded: "In the life of the saints, technically so called, the spiritual faculties are strong, but what gives the impression of extravagance proves usually, on examination, to be a relative deficiency of intellect."[5] For many of the Jewish saints it is not so much a matter of deficiency of intellect as of application in a different sphere of religious life.

RATIONAL VERSUS SAINTLY

The life and work of Bahya Ibn Pakudah is illustrative in this connection. Bahya was certainly no anti-intellectual. He was a learned *dayan* (judge) as well as a distinguished philosopher. The first section of his *Hovot ha-Levavot* is one of the foremost medieval sources of rational inquiry into the existence and nature of God. (Pious readers of the book throughout the ages, bewildered by the rationalistic note, tended to skip this chapter entirely to concentrate on the succeeding *saintly* chapters.) Yet, in his introduction Bahya states that he was moved to compose the work because of the marked absence in Jewish literature of a systematic treatment of "the duties of the heart," as opposed to "the duties of the limbs"–that is, the practical laws and observances of Judaism. Bahya observes, "It is related of one of the sages that he would sit in the company of others until half the day but once he was left on his own he would say, 'Give us the hidden light'."[6]

Another sage was once asked a question regarding the divorce laws. It concerned a case that could occur only very infrequently. The sage replied:

> My dear man! You ask about a matter that will be of no harm to you if you remain ignorant of it. Are you, then, familiar with all the topics that you are obliged to know, of those precepts of which you have no right to remain ignorant and regarding which you must never disobey, that you can spare the time to think about unusual problems from which you will obtain no advantage for your Torah and your faith, and which can contribute nothing towards the rectification of your character defects? Behold, I solemnly swear that for the past thirty-five years I have been occupied in the study of those precepts of the Torah I am required to know, and you are aware of how much trouble I have taken in my studies and of the many books I possess and yet my thoughts have never turned to inquire of the subject you have raised.

He continued in this vein to rebuke his questioner and put him to shame for his attitude. Another sage said:

> I have spent twenty-five years in the improvement of my actions. . . . I once asked one of those with pretensions to be considered a sage regarding this topic to which I have alluded, namely, the wisdom of the conscience, *hokhmat ha-matzpun* (the wisdom of that which is concealed). His reply was to the effect that the tradition we have received from our fathers and teachers is a substitute for reflection on these and similar topics. But, I retorted, such an attitude is appropriate only for one who is incapable of sustained reflection because of the deficiency of his mind and his limited intellectual powers–women and children, for example, or the stupid. But whoever has sufficient intellectual ability to grasp thoroughly whatever he knows of the tradition, yet his indolence and his indifference to God's precepts and His Torah prevent him from

reflecting on these topics, he will be punished for it and be blamed for his neglect.

Luzzatto's *Mesillat Yesharim*[7] was probably influenced by Bahya in the following passage:

> In speaking of wisdom, Solomon said: "If thou seekest her as silver and searchest for her as for hidden treasures, then shalt thou understand the fear of the Lord" (Proverbs 2:4–5). He did not say: "Then shalt thou understand philosophy, astronomy, medicine, the Codes, the *Halakhot*" but "Then shalt thou understand the fear of the Lord."

TRADITIONAL LEARNING AND ATTACHMENT TO GOD

The conflict between the saintly ideal and traditional learning came to the fore during the struggle between the *hasidim* and *mitnaggedim* in the eighteenth century. The reasons for the traditional rabbis' opposition to Hasidism were both social and theological, but a major issue was the hasidic substitution of the ideal of *devekut* (attachment to God) as the supreme aim of the religious life for the study of the Torah as the traditional supreme aim. It was not only that Hasidism had inverted the traditional scale of values, in placing the life of prayer higher than the life devoted to Torah study[8] or that the *hasidim* were constantly accused of being ignorant of the traditional learning.[9] On a deeper level, the conflict was about the transformation by the *hasidim* of study itself. For them the study of Torah was more a devotional than an intellectual pursuit.[10] The traditionalists relied on the talmudic teaching (*Pesahim* 50b) that a man should study the Torah even out of ulterior motives (*she-lo lishmah*), for eventually this would lead to study with pure motivation (*lishmah*).

The *hasidim* on the other hand tended to be very suspicious of scholars who, they maintained, studied only to gain wealth or fame, making a career of their religion. Moreover, for the *hasidim* the doctrine of Torah *lishmah* (Torah for its own sake) meant study for the sake of God, as a devotional exercise; whereas the disciple of the Gaon of Vilna, R. Hayyim of Volozhyn, sought to demonstrate in his *Nefesh ha-Hayyim* that Torah *lishmah* means, rather, studying for the sake of the Torah.[11] R. Hayyim observed that if the student is to master the difficult texts he studies, then he must concentrate on the texts themselves rather than on God. He may come to know God if he applies the *devekut* ideal while he studies, but he will never know Torah. If study deserves to be designated as such, the student must be fully absorbed, to the exclusion of anything other than the topic studied.

Even the kabbalists were not spared in the hasidic pursuit of the *devekut* ideal. It is true that the kabbalists were engaged in the study of a mystical system also held by the *hasidim,* to be the revealed word of God, a very important aspect of Torah study. Yet unless this study becomes a devotional exercise, the *devekut* ideal is frustrated. The eighteenth-century hasidic master, Meshullam Phoebus of Zbarazh,[12] quotes in this connection a statement by the master Menahem Mendel of Premyslani (b. 1728) in which there is an overturning of the two subjects of study–*nigleh,* "the revealed things," and *nistar,* "the secret things." In the tradition, the former refers to the study of Bible and Talmud, the latter to the mysteries of the Kabbalah. For Menahem Mendel *nistar* refers to religious experience, whereas *nigleh* embraces the study of the Kabbalah, a higher pursuit, to be sure, but not the highest for the *hasid. Nistar* refers to something impossible to communicate to others, the taste of food, for example, which cannot be conveyed to one who has never tasted that food. So it is with regard to the love and fear of the Creator, blessed be He. It is impossible to convey to another how this love is in the heart. This is what is meant by *nistar.* But how can it possibly be correct to refer to the Kabbalah as *nistar?* Whoever wishes to study the Kabbalah has the books open to him. If he cannot understand the books, he is simply an ignoramus for whom the Talmud and the Tosafists would also be *nistar.* But the meaning of *nistarot* (the secret things) everywhere in the Zohar and the writings of the *Ari,* of blessed memory, is that these are all understood in the sense of *devekut* to the Creator."

In a trenchant critique of the scholars of his day, Meshullam Phoebus writes:[13]

> They know nothing of what attachment (*devekut*) to God means and nothing of what love and fear mean. For they imagine that their studies

> in themselves constitute attachment to God and that these in themselves are the love and fear of God. But how can that be? It is well known that many of the scholars are guilty of fornication, Heaven forbid, and are notorious sinners. It happens also to be true that many Gentiles study our Torah. How, then, can this be considered attachment to God? For one who is attached to God in love and fear cannot possibly commit even the slightest sin, to say nothing of a serious sin, God forbid, and to say nothing of attachment to some lust, God forbid. For, surely, God is holy and separate from all matter. . . . How can there possibly be attachment by means of the Torah in the manner in which they conduct themselves and despise prayer? The truth of the matter is that they only learn by rote in order to be considered wise.

In the late 1970s a hasidic master, Zevi Hirsch Rosenbaum,[14] could still bemoan the fact that even in hasidic *yeshivot,* the saintly way as described by Meshullam Phoebus is no longer followed, while the mitnaggedic attitude toward learning is admired.

> For we have a tradition from all the *Zaddikim,* our fathers and our teachers, that only the type of Torah and of the love and fear of God that follows the way of the light of our eyes, the Baal Shem Tov, may his merits protect us, by whose lips we live, can bring near our true redemption (not as those who go astray, to be envious of ordinary scholars, and this is the reason why there is a daily increase of speakers and guides in the hasidic *yeshivot,* those who do not walk in the trusted way of Hasidism). As it has been truly said by the holy divine, Rabbi Meshullam Phoebus of Zbarazh, of blessed memory.

OTHER HASIDIC VIEWS

It would be a mistake to imagine, however, that all the hasidic masters departed from the traditional scholarly ideal. Thus the hasidic master Yitzhak Eisik of Komarno (1805–1874), in *Notzer Hesed,* comments on the Mishnah (*Avot* 1:13) where it is said: "One who does not study deserves to die; and he who makes a worldly use of the crown of the Torah shall waste away."

> He said, "One who does not study." This is a warning against stupid *Hasidut.* It is perfectly true that the main thing is to study the Torah for

> its own sake and in order to be in a state of attachment (*devekut*) to God. But such is on a most elevated plane, and it is impossible for a man to arrive all at once to the stage of *lishmah* (for its own sake). A man is bound to study the Torah out of ulterior motives (*she-lo lishmah*) at first until his character has become sufficiently refined to enable him to take delight in the Torah. Even when the Torah is studied out of ulterior motives, its inner light will eventually produce a worthier motivation. But the stupid try all at once to seize hold of this inner light, and since they are unworthy of it they give up Torah study entirely. For they do not want to study with ulterior motives since they are *hasidim,* and as for study for its own sake this is quite beyond them at the time. In order to negate this type of stupidity–it is verily stupidity, since the main thing in life is to study the Torah, and there is nothing of greater value in the whole world–the Tanna remarks: "He who does not study deserves to die," by the hand of Heaven, since he has no part in eternal life (the life of the Torah). "And he who makes a worldly use of the crown of the Torah shall find it transformed." He who makes use of the king's scepter for his own benefit, by studying the Torah with ulterior motives, will nevertheless be transformed, as it is said: "But they that wait for the Lord shall renew their strength" (Isaiah 40:31), for out of study with ulterior motivation, study out of pure motive will emerge [as well as] holy stages of worship. But one who does not study at all has nothing to be transformed and will remain on high in a state of acute embarrassment."

Here we have a subtle play on words. The Hebrew *halaf* is generally translated as *waste away.* But R. Yitzhak Eisik has rendered it as *will be transformed,* the same word (*yahalifu*) used in the Isaiah text. In the process he has himself "transformed" the whole concept, coming very close to the non-hasidic doctrine of Torah study and close to agreement with R. Hayyim of Volozhyn.

The hasidic master Abraham of Sochachow (1839–1910) was a renowned talmudist as well as a hasidic rebbe. The introduction to his *Egley Tal* includes an interesting excursus on this topic. After quoting the rabbinic statement that one should study the Torah even if the motivation is less than pure, this author continues:

> As I speak I must recall having heard of some folk who wander astray in the matter of study of our holy Torah, arguing that one who studies

> creatively and enjoys his studies is not considered to be one who studies *lishmah,* as much as one, in a simple plain manner, in which there is no enjoyment but the study is engaged in out of religious obligation. They argue that one who studies and enjoys it brings his own enjoyment into his studies. The truth, however, is that such an attitude is notoriously false. On the contrary, it belongs to the very concept of Torah study that the student should enjoy and take delight in his studies, for then the words of the Torah are absorbed in his blood and since he enjoys studying the Torah, he becomes attached (*davuk!*) to the Torah. The holy Zohar states that both the good inclination and the evil inclination can only grow through joy, the good inclination through the joy of Torah study, evil inclination through etc. But if you argue that where the studies are enjoyed it is *she-lo lishmah,* or, at best, both *she-lo lishmah* and *lishmah,* it would follow that the joy one has in study diminishes the force of the precept and reduces its illumination, so how can the good inclination grow as a result? Since the good inclination grows thereby it obviously follows joy in study is an integral part of the precept. I admit that when one studies not at all to fulfill the obligation but solely for the enjoyment he has when he studies that it is, indeed, called *she-lo lishmah,* just as when one eats *matzah* on Passover not in order to fulfill the precept but simply because he likes the taste of unleavened bread. But when one studies in order to fulfill the precept and, at the same time, he enjoys his studies, it is called Torah *lishmah* and is all of it holy since the very enjoyment is in itself the fulfillment of a religious obligation.

Many other hasidic masters were noted talmudists. Aaron Soresky (*Marbitzey Torah me-Olam ha-Hasidut*) has published a six-volume account of these masters, and others can easily be added.

The tension to which we have referred surfaced again in the Lithuanian Musar movement and the polemics against the movement on the part of the traditionalist rabbis.[15] The Musarists argued that without the addition of moralistic, religious exercises of the kind practiced in the movement, the study of the Torah is ineffective. The opponents of the movement, on the other hand, refused to accept the notion that the study of the Torah by itself is ineffective in ennobling man and in helping him overcome his lusts and passions. R. Hayyim Soloveitchick is reported to have said that Musar is helpful to the sick soul much as castor oil is beneficial to one who suffers from stomach trouble. But whoever heard of a healthy person taking castor oil?

3

THE MAKING OF A SAINT

Accounts of how *Hasidut* is to be cultivated are few and far between in the literature of Jewish piety. A number of saintly rules (*hanhagot*) were set forth in various periods, but these are, in the main, regulations for those advanced on the saintly way rather than in the nature of advice to aspirants for the saintly vocation.

STRIVING FOR SAINTHOOD

It would seem that, for a number of reasons, the Jewish masters are comparatively silent on the question of how to attain to sainthood. First, one can see a marked reserve in the advocacy of saintliness as a goal for which to strive. *Hasidut,* like happiness, cannot be pursued. It is either present or absent. Where it is absent, no amount of conscious striving for *Hasidut* will bring that ideal any nearer. The very striving negates the saintly aim because it displays a lack of humility. When a man implies that he could become a saint if he made the effort, he has already denied an essential saintly characteristic. And when *Hasidut* is present, the last person to be aware of it is the saint himself. The *hasid* is, or should be, so aware of his own shortcomings that he considers it an impertinence to offer counsel to others in the matter. Second, Judaism emphasizes the deed–*doing* the will of God. Even with regard to what Bahya calls "the duties of the heart," the emphasis is on obligation. There are obligations to love God and one's neighbor, but there is no precept to become a saint. Third, the *hasidim,* like the mystics (they are often identical), tend to be reluctant to bare their souls to others. Scholem[1] offers this reticence as a reason for the fact that there are so few Jewish mystical testimonies of an intimate, personal nature.[2]

THE SAINTLY PATH

Nevertheless, there are a number of works that, although of value to ordinary pious Jews with no saintly ambitions, were actually compiled as guides to saintly living and used as such. A notable example is the *Sefer Hasidim,* produced by the *Hasidey Ashkenaz.* This work not only provides illustrations of the saintly path but also refers to the spiritual guide who advises aspirants on how to reach the ranks of the saints. For instance, after quoting the talmudic passage (*Berakhot* 34b), in which confession of sin to others is frowned upon, the work goes on to observe that this is not the case when confession is made to a discreet sage who can instruct the sinner in how to do penance for his sins so that he might inherit eternal life.[3] (We noted earlier that repentance is an essential element of the saintly life for the *Hasidey Ashkenaz.*) Dan is far too sweeping when he states that these *hasidim* entirely rejected the Christian forms of confession, even though he admits that their doctrine of repentance was strongly influenced by Christian practice.[4] As a matter of fact, the *Sefer Hasidim* even instructs the mentor (*ha-moreh*) in how to proceed when the sinner confesses his sins:[5]

> First, the mentor should ask the sinner if he truly regrets having sinned. If he replies in the affirmative, the mentor should say to him, if the sin was with a woman, "If you are truly sorry, you must keep away from that woman, neither speaking to her nor seeing her for a whole year. Do this at first, and then if you can keep to it I shall tell you what to do in order to erase the sin," for no sin can be removed without mortification, as it is said, "Lo, this (burning coal) has touched thy lips; and thine

> iniquity is taken away, and thy sin expiated" (Isaiah 6:7). If the sinner says, "Give me a different penance; this one is too hard for me," he is not to be heeded, for repentance is only possible when the sinner turns from his former deeds and makes a fence around them. . . . After this, the mentor should give him the aforementioned penance, i.e., to forbid him to enjoy anything that comes from a woman's hand, except that of his own wife. When the sinner fasts in atonement for his sins, the mentor should flog him severely in private, for all voluntary pain the sinner takes upon himself is counted as the suffering that brings atonement in its wake. Consequently, fasting is good since it is beneficial to the body, and also almsgiving to ward off punishment. Since he is deserving of death, he should gain pardon by bringing new life to the souls of the hungry and he should revive them.

Scattered throughout the book are tales of the saints (variously called *hasid, hakham, tzaddik*), with the aim of instructing the would-be *hasid* on the implications of saintly conduct. A *hasid* was once insulted, and the community wished to impose a ban on the offender, but the saint refused to allow it. When the people protested that if they overlooked the offense they would be encouraging disrespectful behavior, the saint replied that on the contrary, if his attitude were adopted, it would reduce strife and hatred through his example of patient resignation.[6]

Another saint (here *hakham*) similarly refused to punish a man who had insulted him, saying, "It was my sins that brought about my sufferings, and if there is to be punishment, I am the one to be punished."[7] Another hot tempered saint (here *tzaddik*) used to curse those who insulted him but was filled with remorse once his anger had waned. When he turned for advice to his mentor, the *hakham* advised him that whenever he was tempted to curse someone, he should say, "Whatever curses I hurl at that man's head should come upon me," and this would keep his temper in check.[8]

The word *hasid* is connected to the word *hasadim* (kindnesses) and also, with a considerable degree of license, to a word meaning *white,* to yield the thought that the true *hasid* will not retaliate even if he is so insulted that his face turns white with rage.[9] The *hasid* is expected to be excessively strict in his observance of ritual. If, for instance, there is a debate among the sages in matters of ritual law, the *hasid* should always follow the stricter view, even when the law is decided in favor of the more lenient view.[10] The saint is always in doubt about whether he deserves to enjoy eternal bliss in the Hereafter. The wiser and more righteous a man is, the greater is his uncertainty that he will be allowed to enter Paradise.[11]

In his *Sodey Razayya,* Eleazar of Worms (c. 1162–c. 1230), the foremost disciple of Judah He-Hasid, provides a remarkable guide to the love of God, intended to prepare the would-be initiate into the mysteries of the *Merkavah,* the divine chariot seen by the prophet Ezekiel.[12] Part of this is given here in translation:

> Now I shall instruct you how to love God, blessed be He, and then I shall write out for you the secret of the *Merkavah.* "Let a man always be subtle in the fear of God" (*Berakhot* 17a). The meaning is that he should reflect on the subtleties and glories of the world, how, for example, a mortal king orders his soldiers to do battle. Even though they know full well that they may be killed in battle, yet they obey him in their fear of him, even though they know that their fear of him will not last forever, since the day will come when he will die and perish, and they can flee to another country. How much more so, then, should a man fear the King of Kings, the Holy One, blessed be He, and walk in His ways, for He is everywhere and looks upon the wicked and the good. Whenever a man sees companies of righteous men, he should attach himself to them that he might have a portion among them. . . .
>
> The root of saintliness (*Hasidut*) is for man to go beyond the letter of the law. . . . The root of the fear of the Lord is when a man desires something and yet gives up the pleasure his evil inclination craves because he fears the Lord. It is not that he fears punishment in this world or the next. His fear is that he may not be perfect before God, whom he loves. . . . The root of love is the love of the Lord. The soul is full of love, bound with bonds of love in great joy. Such rapture drives away from his heart every bodily pleasure and worldly delight. The powerful joy of love seizes his heart so that at all times he thinks only of how to do God's will. The pleasures he derives from his children and the company of his wife are as nothing in comparison with his love of God. Imagine a young man who has been without a woman for a very long time. He longs for her, his heart burning for her. Imagine the great love and desire when at last he has intercourse with her and how much pleasure he

obtains from his sperm shooting out like an arrow. All this is as nothing compared with his desire to do the will of God, to bring merit to others, to sanctify himself, to offer up his very life in love. . . . The love of Heaven in his heart is like the flame attached to the coal. He does not gaze at women, he does not engage in frivolous talk, but he concerns himself only to do the will of God and he sings songs in order to become filled with joy in the love of God. . . .

Carry out all your good deeds in secret and walk humbly with thy God. But if you do it in order that they might learn from your example, then do it in the presence of others. . . . Be energetic in performing good deeds and never speak vain things.

Bahya Ibn Pakudah's *Duties of the Heart,* a complete guide to saintly conduct, quotes illustrative tales of "a certain *hasid.*" But the interesting feature here is that, as scholars have noted, the reference is often not to a Jewish saint but to a Sufi saint. The influence of Sufism is seen throughout Bahya's work, including even the title *Duties of the Heart.* The work is divided into ten chapters. With the exception of the first, on the nature of God and the rational proofs for His existence, each of the other chapters ("gates") describes a particular saintly virtue and how it is to be cultivated. Thus there are gates of:

- examination (how to come to the love of God through an examination of how His goodness operates)
- Divine worship
- trust in God
- complete sincerity and integrity in God's service
- humility
- repentance
- self-scrutiny
- abstinence
- love of God

Each gate is divided into sub-chapters, which lead the reader step by step on the road to saintliness. Bahya's *Duties of the Heart* is one of the most widely read of Jewish devotional works. It has been translated into Yiddish, a sure sign of its popularity among the unlearned as well as the learned. Nevertheless, the book is essentially elitist. It is for the few who aspire to saintly living rather than for the masses, from whom the author expects far less.

OTHER GUIDES FOR SAINTLY LIVING

Guides for saintly living in the mystical vein were produced in, or under the influence of, the Safed school of kabbalists: *Tomer Devorah,* by Moses Cordovero (1522–1570); *Reshit Hokhmah,* by Elijah de Vidas (d. c. 1593); *Shaarey Kedushah,* by Hayyim Vital (1542–1620); *Sheney Luhot ha-Berit,* by Isaiah Horowitz (d. 1630).

Cordovero's *Tomer Devorah* (Palm Tree of Deborah) is a kabbalistic text on the understanding of the doctrine of *Imitatio Dei.* The mystical adept is expected to reflect in his conduct the manifestations of each of the ten *Sefirot,* the powers in the Godhead, on which the kabbalists dwell at length. For instance, in Cordovero's scheme, the mystic should strive to emulate the *Sefirah Hokhmah* (wisdom) by endeavoring to assist all God's creatures, just as on high this quality is extended to all. He should, therefore, despise no created thing, neither plant nor animal, unless it is unavoidable (i.e., when it is for human use). Similarly, of the *Sefirah Malkhut,* the lowest of the *Sefirot,* in which some of the others find lodging, so to speak, the mystic should have this principle in mind when he emulates *Malkhut* on high by providing hospitality for wayfarers in his home. Cordovero concludes:

> This is the daily cycle to be in accord with the cycle of the *Sefirot,* so that he is ever attached to the particular illumination dominant at the time. This counsel is chiefly contained in the opening section on Genesis in the Zohar, the rest being contained in other places in the Zohar. And this is a most comprehensive method by means of which one can bind himself always in holiness so that the crown of the *Shekhinah* never departs from his head.

De Vidas's *Reshit Hokhmah* (Beginning of Wisdom) is a mystical treatise similar to, but more comprehensive than, Cordovero's. The work was also published in abbreviated form by Jacob Poyetto under the title *Kitzur Reshit Hokhmah.*[13] It consists of "gates" subdivided into chapters, and it describes in rich detail how the adept can attain the fear of God, the love of God, repentance, holiness, and humility–the five essentials of the saintly life.

Vital's *Shaarey Kedushah* (Gates of Holiness) aims to describe the steps to holy living. The use of the word *gates* in these works is revealing: They open the gates through which the novice is to pass in order to realize his saintly ambitions. In the printed editions of Vital's work there are only three gates, but Vital's manuscript includes a fourth gate, in which the adept is advised on how to proceed in order to attain the gift of the holy spirit, *ruah ha-kodesh.* This gate was left in manuscript by the printers, who evidently considered this final aim to be beyond the reach of their contemporaries.

Horowitz's *Sheney Luhot ha-Berit* (The Two Tablets of Stone, abbreviated *Shelah*) is a vast compendium of Jewish teachings, including a running commentary to the Pentateuch and a section on talmudic methodology. But scattered throughout the book are passages in which guidance is offered to those eager to tread the saintly path.

The most detailed manual for saintly living, however, is Luzzatto's *Mesillat Yesharim* (Path of the Upright), based, as noted earlier, on the ladder of spiritual ascent described by R. Phinehas b. Yair: "The knowledge of the Torah leads to watchfulness, watchfulness to zeal, zeal to cleanness, cleanness to abstinence, abstinence to purity, purity to saintliness, saintliness to humility, humility to the fear of sin, and the fear of sin to holiness." Luzzatto has four chapters on *Hasidut,* exploring its meaning, its various aspects, the deliberations necessary for its cultivation, and the process by which it is attained.[14] In the first of these chapters, Luzzatto once again stresses that saintliness is a science, requiring severe intellectual application:

> In truth, the nature of saintliness requires considerable explanation. There are numerous habits and practices which pass for most people as saintliness but which are in reality nothing more than the rude and inchoate forms of this trait. This is the case because those of whom these habits are characteristic lack the power of true understanding and reflection. They have not troubled and failed to understand clearly and correctly the way of the Lord. They have practiced saintliness according

to the course of conduct they hit upon at first thought. They have not delved deeply into things, nor have they weighed them in the scales of wisdom. Such people render the very savor of saintliness repellent to the average person, as well as to the more intelligent. They give the impression that saintliness depends on foolish practices that are contrary to reason and to common sense, like reciting numerous supplicatory prayers and long confessions, or weeping and genuflections, or afflicting oneself with strange torments that are liable to bring one to death's door, such as fasting and ablutions in ice and snow. Though some of these practices may serve as an expiation for certain sins, while others may be fit for ascetics, they cannot form the basis of saintliness. The best of these practices may be associated with saintliness; nevertheless, saintliness itself, properly understood, is something far more profound. Saintliness should be reared upon great wisdom and upon the adjustment of conduct to the aims worthy of the truly wise. Only the wise can truly grasp the nature of saintliness; as our sages said, "The ignorant man cannot be a *hasid*" (*Avot* 2:5).

HOMILIES OF THE HASIDIC MASTERS

Beshtian Hasidism uses the works of Bahya, Luzzatto, and others (especially de Vidas and Horowitz). In this movement each of the masters sought to map out both his own individual way and his conception of the hasidic way in general. Basically, all hasidic literature consists of counsel for the attainment of *Hasidut,* at least in its Beshtian version, although much of the literature is ambiguous as to whether the way in all its fullness is reserved for the *zaddik* or is intended to apply to every sincere *hasid.* Even the tales of the *zaddikim,* so prominent a feature of the literature, were intended, in part, to provide examples of saintly conduct for emulation by the *hasid* or, where emulation is considered inappropriate, for the *hasid* to draw lessons from for the conduct of his own (admittedly inferior) strivings. But the most important presentation of the saintly way is to be found in the largely nonsystematic *torot* (doctrines) of the masters. These hasidic homilies number in the hundreds, amounting to a vast library of spiritual guidance. The hasidic devotee Nahman of Tcherin compiled, in the last century, two anthologies of the teachings of the early masters:

Lashon Hasidim, on the teachings of the Baal Shem Tov and his disciples, and *Derekh Hasidim,* on the teachings of the Maggid and his disciples. The material in these anthologies is arranged under headings that are clearly directed toward the goal of providing detailed instruction for saintly living, although, in a sense, such systematic treatment is foreign to the forms of hasidic teaching in which ideas burst spontaneously forth as the *zaddik* seeks to guide his *hasidim.*

The teachings are arranged alphabetically (in Hebrew) in these two anthologies. There are sections on:

the love of God, faith
sincerity
eating for the sake of Heaven
humility
devekut
the practice of solitude
joy in God's service
suffering
trust in God
spiritual counseling
the role of the *zaddik*
repentance, peace, and tranquility

Only very occasionally do we find glimpses into the more personal, intimate, spiritual progress of the hasidic masters. These masters, following earlier mystical writings, tend to think of "stages" (*madregot*) in spiritual advance. (The saint who has advanced far on the road to spiritual elevation is known as a *baal madregah,* "master of stages.") Again following earlier kabbalistic writings, there is an awareness that there is retreat as well as advance in the spiritual life, descent as well as ascent. There is knowledge of what Christian mystics call "the dark night of the soul." The kabbalistic term used for elevation of the soul, for the state where joy reigns supreme, is *gadlut de-mohin* (greatness of mind). For the darker mood, where all is obscure and remote and the divine seems inaccessible, the other kabbalistic term is used, *katnut de-mohin* (smallness of mind). These terms are based on the kabbalistic doctrine of the *Sefirot,* which similarly delineates harmonious periods and less than harmonious periods, so that the ebb and flow of faith and spiritual striving mirrors the Sefirotic realms.

For instance, there is the homily on Jacob's dream of the ladder (Genesis 28:10–11) by Moses Hayyim Ephraim of Sudlikow, grandson of the Baal Shem Tov, in his *Degel Mahaney Efrayim.*[15] The angels of God whom Jacob saw ascending and descending the ladder were the *zaddikim,* who did, indeed, descend from their elevated state from time to time, but their very descent was for the purpose of still higher ascents. This author quotes his grandfather:

> Contained in this passage is the secret of greatness and smallness. The saying of my master, my grandfather, his soul is in Eden, his memory for a blessing, is well known. "The living creatures run to and fro" (Ezekiel 1:14) and it is impossible for a man always to remain at the same stage, but he is obliged to ascend and descend. His descent is, however, for the purpose of further ascent. For when a man considers that he is in the state of smallness, he prays to the Lord, as it is said, "But from thence ye will seek the Lord thy God; and thou shalt find Him" (Deuteronomy 4:28). The meaning of "from thence" is, from the place in which you find yourself, as my master, my grandfather, his soul is in Eden, his memory for a blessing, has said.

That is, the foot of the ladder is set upon the earth, lowly and remote from Heaven, but for that very reason its head reaches to the Heavens. This is why, concludes Moses Hayyim Ephraim, it is said of the patriarchs that they went *up* out of Egypt. They emerged even stronger in their spiritual life through their descent into the Egypt of narrowness and spiritual constriction.

This idea of spiritual ebb and flow is similarly appended to the narrative of Jacob's dream in the first published hasidic work, *Toledot Yaakov Yosef.*[16] The ladder, with its foot on the ground and its head reaching toward Heaven, is the *zaddik* (the term used here is *talmid hakham*). In his elevated stage the upper worlds are influenced by his deeds. But perforce the *zaddik,* too, has his times of spiritual descent. This descent of the *zaddik* is necessary if he is to associate with ordinary folk whom he can lead to greater heights. When Jacob saw that the sun had set (Genesis 28:11)–that is, that he had fallen from his elevated stage (*madregah*)–he became distressed, but he was promised that God would prevent his suffering spiritual contamination through his association with the masses. In a further interpretation of the dream, the author sees the ladder (the *zaddik*) standing firmly on the ground (i.e., involved in worldly pursuits) but always with his head in the Heavens, his thoughts always on God, in order to unite the worlds below with the worlds on high.

A later hasidic master, Zevi Elimelech of Dinov (1785–1841), on the other hand, holds that it is wrong for a man consciously to desire a high degree of elevation of the soul.[17] This master comments on the verse "Neither shalt thou go up by steps unto my altar, that thy nakedness be not uncovered thereon" (Exodus 20:23):

> To my mind there is a hint in this precept that a man should not (consciously) seek elevation and high stages even in God's service, namely, to wish to attain to the holy spirit or to wish Elijah to appear to him and the like. If God does honor him with some elevated stage (*madregah*), he should give thanks to the Lord, who is good, but he himself should not seek great things. Rather should he serve the Lord in love and fear and simplicity, like a son who strives on his father's behalf whom he loves more than himself. But if the idea enters his mind that he is worthy to attain to elevated stages, then, God forbid, he will be scrutinized and his shame uncovered. Consequently, let a man not seek consciously for this but hope in the Lord and do good, namely, that which the Torah commands us to do. It is otherwise with regard to the attainment of the holy spirit and the appearance of Elijah and such like. We are not commanded concerning these in the Torah, yet when a man is honored in this manner from Heaven he is then obliged to give thanks to the Lord for His gracious and free gifts. This is the meaning of "Neither shalt thou go up by steps," namely, your shame will be revealed that you do not really care to serve God for His own sake, like a son who strives etc., but you seek only your own greatness. Understand this well.

> As I speak of this topic, I must show you that even when a man is worthy to attain to high spiritual stages (*madregot*) he is sometimes prevented from attaining these for some reason known only to God.

Zevi Elimelech adds that one of the reasons that God withholds His spiritual gifts, even from those who deserve them, may be that God uses the saint's merits to protect his generation, so that for the saint to use them in order to acquire higher spiritual stages for himself is selfish and uncaring. It is not too difficult to read between the lines here. The hasidic master is conscious that he cannot simultaneously act as a spiritual guide to his more humble followers and pursue his own path to saintly living in isolation, that he might receive the heavenly favor of spiritual elevation.

The dangers of aiming too high are stressed also by the hasidic master Abraham Joshua Heschel of Apta (d. 1825) in his *Ohev Yisrael.*[18] Quoting the same verse as Zevi Elimelech, Abraham Joshua comments on Rashi's remark regarding the first verse of Leviticus that before God commanded Moses, He called him.

> You should know that Rashi teaches us here a great principle of the Torah, namely, just as Moses did not draw near to converse with the *Shekhinah* until he was invited, so, too, the man who wishes to ascend to the Lord stage by stage must await the call for him to proceed to the next stage. For true worship is when man *serves* God and has no real desire to attain to any elevated stage unless he is first invited and coerced from on high because such a stage is required for the benefit of his community. Now we have seen with our own eyes many *hasidim* who become insane, God forbid, or afflicted with melancholia. How could such things have happened? Surely it cannot have been, God forbid, because of the Torah they studied. On the contrary, study of the Torah makes the heart ever more joyful, which is why the rabbis disallow a mourner to study the Torah (*Taanit* 30b). Nor can it be the result of carrying out the precepts, since the statutes of the Lord are right, rejoicing the heart (Psalm 19:9). But the reason for it is that they are men who wish to ascend to the Lord but cannot find the ladder of ascent. For they do not serve God at a gradual pace and seize hold of that which is not for them, having received neither invitation nor permission from on high. And there are those who serve God with the sole intention of becoming one

> who has reached an elevated stage (*baal madregah*). Concerning this it is said (Exodus 20:23) "Neither shalt thou go up by steps unto my altar," namely in order to become one of the elite and one who has reached an elevated stage, "that thy nakedness be not uncovered thereon," as we have seen, they become afflicted with melancholia. Not so is the way of the perfect servants of God, who have no wish to reach any elevated stages. And even though we see that they have attained such stages, it is only because they have been coerced into it for the good of the community. Let a man take heed of this and let him not persist in breaking through to God, for many tried to follow R. Simeon b. Yohai and they failed (*Berakhot* 35b).

THE FALL OF THE SAINT

R. Yitzhak Eisik of Komarno, in the introduction to his *Hekhal ha-Berakhah,* writes that the spiritual fall of the zaddik can come about as a result of persecution by opponents of the saint so that he is led to doubt whether the way he has chosen is correct. R. Yitzhak Eisik's father-in-law told him that the renowned R. Levi Yitzhak of Berditchev was so persecuted by the *mitnaggedim* that in 1793 he suffered a nervous breakdown. The saint was helped back to mental stability by his disciple R. Israel of Koznitz (1733–1814). R. Yitzhak Eisik's remarks merit quotation as a very unusual document on the tensions inherent in the saintly life:

> They persecuted our holy teachers, as they did to the holy man, wonder of his generation, our rabbi, R. Levi Yitzhak, of blessed memory, of whom my father-in-law related that they used to upset him grievously without end. In the year 5553 (1793) so severe was his distress that he fell from his elevated stage (*nafal mi-madregato*) into a fit of depression (*marah shehorah*), and he used to pray out of a little prayerbook at great speed with his mind slightly unhinged. All this is well known. My father-in-law, R. Abraham Mordecai of Pinchow, told me that the holy Maggid of Koznitz, R. Levi Yitzhak's disciple, helped him a great deal. He said that in the normal course of events they would not have allowed him to fall from his stage, God forbid, but in that year there was an attack on him in Heaven as well because of his attack on the Heavenly princes so that they could not help him. My father-in-law visited him

> after these events in the year 5554 (1794) to find him restored to his elevated stage, possessing wonderful illuminations and great stages (*madregot*). He stayed with him for almost a year, learning from him Torah and how to love and fear God. He became like a glowing fire and yet was made to feel small by those etc. [i.e., by his own disciples]. He summoned my father-in-law and said to him, "Observe, my son, I cast lots to determine whether they are unfit to associate with me because they belong to the mixed multitude or whether they are worthy men and the unworthiness is mine. But every time the lot so fell that it determined it was they and not I who were unworthy." We have witnessed many in our generation who, because they were distressed in this fashion, fell from grace and suffered a descent, for their soul could not endure it, as happened to a rabbi who lived near to a big city. He was a disciple of R. Elimelech and other great masters in Israel. Also with regard to our master, life of our soul, the Baal Shem Tov, it once happened that because they made him feel small he actually did feel small, etc., until one of his foremost disciples appeared at that moment to stand in awe in his presence. When he addressed him as "master and teacher," he was restored. . . .

The master who is said to have helped R. Levi Yitzhak, R. Israel of Koznitz, was evidently bothered himself by spiritual lulls and lack of obvious spiritual progress. R. Israel bares his soul in his *Avodat Yisrael* in a comment on the use of the word *sheretz* (Leviticus 11:43) to denote a creeping thing.[19] *Sheretz,* he says, is connected with the word meaning "to run." Because they have tiny legs, these creatures run swiftly without getting very far. He applies this metaphor to spiritual progress. A Jew who falls from his stage runs speedily to return to God, and he experiences a sense of spiritual achievement. Once he has reached the elevated stage, however, his progress is bound to be less discernible. R. Israel tells of a dream he had in which he asked the Baal Shem Tov why, when he first began to follow the hasidic way, his progress was always evident, whereas now, from the point of view of spiritual advance, one day seems exactly like another. The Baal Shem Tov replied in the dream that a youngster makes obvious rapid progress in his studies because it is all new to him. The mature student is already accustomed to making great progress, and although his daily strides are far greater than those of the novice, his progress is less apparent because of his familiarity with his subject. R. Israel concludes: "This is wondrous wisdom. By means of this idea you can come to understand many things regarding *gadlut* and *katnut.*"

As is the case with other aspects of saintliness, there is no uniform view in the sources. But it is clear that the masters saw their aim as extremely difficult, and the saintly life as one of ebb and flow, *gadlut* and *katnut.*

4

SAINTLY EXTRAVAGANCE

The saintly character is prone to excess by its very nature. That which religious convention would consider extravagance, the saint considers normal and natural conduct; he is merely pursuing his chosen path.

William James, in *The Varieties of Religious Experience,* has a chapter entitled "Saintliness,"[1] in which he gives a number of illustrations from the history of Christian devotion of extravagant behavior on the part of some of the saints. For instance, M. Vinnaney, the curé of Ars, in his quest for holiness, vowed that he would never smell a flower, never drink when parched with thirst, never drive away a fly, never show disgust before a repugnant object, never complain of anything that had to do with his personal comfort, never sit down, and never lean upon his elbows when kneeling. Saint John of the Cross urged the mortification of the four great natural passions – joy, hope, fear, and grief. The soul, he wrote, should turn always not to that which is most easy, but to that which is hardest; not to what tastes best, but to what is most distasteful; not to what pleases, but to what disgusts; not to will anything, but to will nothing. "Despise yourself," he says, "and wish that others should despise you. Speak to your own disadvantage, and desire others to do the same. Conceive a low opinion of yourself, and find it good when others hold the same." The Blessed Henry Suso wore, for a long time, a hair shirt studded with nails that pierced his flesh. (As we will see, there are parallels to these examples in the literature of Jewish saintliness, except for smelling the flowers–in Judaism it is considered meritorious to smell sweet odors and thank God for them–and inviting disgust–forbidden in Judaism on the basis of the verse "Ye shall not make yourselves detestable" (Leviticus 11:43, which, in its rabbinic interpretation [*Makkot* 17b], includes the prohibition of doing anything that invites disgust). James gives additional examples of this kind of saintly excess and then raises the issue of how this kind of behavior is to be viewed.

James observes[2] that saintly behavior strikes the average religious person as unbalanced. People who have studied the lives of the saints generally ask, "Does one have to be quite so good, so holy, so generous?" But, James continues, in every sphere of life, the determined pursuit of an ideal to the virtual exclusion of other aims results in a lack of proportion and a strong degree of imbalance. One-sidedness is the price the saint has to pay and is ready to pay.

According to James,

> The fruits of religion, in other words, are, like all human products, liable to corruption by excess. Common sense must judge them. It need not blame the votary; but it may be able to praise him only conditionally, as one who acts faithfully according to his lights. He shows us heroism in one way, but the unconditionally good way is that for which no indulgence need be asked.

Somewhat patronizing though it is, this piece of fine Jamesian prose is bound to challenge Jewish readers to consider whether the same problem exists in Judaism. Jewish theologians since the beginning of the last century have tended to see Judaism as always too sane, too balanced, too sweetly reasonable to view the kind of excess of which James speaks as anything but aberration.[3] The Jewish *hasid,* it is frequently claimed, is always a *hakham* (sage), never a fool, not even a fool of God. That such an opinion is as one-sided as the conduct of James's saints must be obvious to the unbiased student of Jewish ideas.

This chapter seeks to cap James's examples with some from Jewish hagiographies, in addition to those already mentioned. Although care has been taken to use only fairly reliable reports, the historicity of the events related is really irrelevant to the inquiry, since the tales of the saints, true or otherwise, are themselves evidence that saintly excesses are not considered excesses at all but are the norm for the saints.

There are numerous examples of this type of wild piety in Beshtian Hasidism, but lest it be argued that this form of saintliness is so way-out as to be completely atypical, we can first note some examples from the camp of the allegedly more sober Litvak–*mitnaggedic* devotees.

HAFETZ HAYYIM

In the recently published guide to Jewish family life, *Mitzvot ha-Bayit,* by Rabbi Joseph D. Epstein,[4] there is a quote from the son of the renowned saint of this school, Israel Meir Kagan (1838–1933),[5] *Hafetz Hayyim.* The son writes:

> Father had no personal friendships with anyone all the days of his life, even though he loved every Jew and especially men learned in the Torah, whom he loved as his very self. Many times did I hear him tell how the daughter of the Vilna Gaon, who lived in another town, once paid a visit to her father. The Gaon inquired after her health and that of her husband and children and then immediately returned to his studies. The daughter began to weep at her father's apparent indifference, but he declared, "I do not have the time" [in Yiddish, *nitoh kein zeit*]. So it is not surprising that father, of blessed memory, had no material friendships with anyone. . . . I once heard him explain the verse "And thou shalt love the Lord thy God with all thy heart" (Deuteronomy 6:5) to mean that the heart should be so filled with the love of God as to leave no room in it for any other loves.

Epstein quotes, too, the remarks of R. Hayyim of Volozhyn, foremost disciple of the Vilna Gaon, on his master: "His separation from all worldly matters was amazing to the extent that he never inquired about the welfare of his children. He never wrote letters of greeting to them and never read the letters he received from them"[6] – one-sidedness with a vengeance. Another teacher Epstein quotes in this connection is R. Alexander Süsskind of Grodno (d. 1793).[7] This Lithuanian saint never kissed his children, never took them in his arms when they were little, and never engaged in idle talk with them lest it result in waste of the time that should be spent in the study of the Torah.

Epstein, evidently conscious of how inhuman it all sounds, observes that he admitted these tales into his guide for everyman only because they set forth the ideal of how far the love of God and His Torah should go. But the ideal is for only the greatest of saints. For ordinary mortals to seek to emulate their conduct would be absurd and morally wrong. Epstein's remarks here tally with those of James on the way in which ordinary folk might approach the excesses of the saints, although Epstein, naturally, does not admit to one-sidedness on the part of his heroes.

YOIZEL HOROWITZ

In approximately 1882, the wife of R. Yoizel Horowitz died in childbirth. (R. Yoizel was a leading figure in the Musar movement and was a disciple of R. Israel Salanter and founder of the Navaradok school of Musar.) For a year and a half thereafter, R. Yoizel lived as a hermit in a hut at the back of his lodgings. He never left his voluntary prison during the whole of that period, not even to go the synagogue. The hut had two holes in the wall, through which pious women would send him food; there was one hole for meat dishes and one for dairy dishes. He became known, scathingly, by the opponents of Musar as "the master of the holes." It is reported that when he needed food, he would ring a bell and place into the hole a slip of paper, on which he would write his meager requirements, so as not to have to converse with anyone during the time of his seclusion. He would regularly immerse himself 300 times in a *mikveh* in the courtyard of the house; that is, he would place his finger in and out of the water 300 times, in obedience to a kabbalistic formula he had discovered. It is said that R. Yoizel would spend at least eighteen hours a day studying the Torah.[8]

ELIMELECH OF LIZENSK

To R. Elimelech of Lizensk (1717–1787), a leading hasidic master, is attributed a series of rules for saints known as *Tzetil Katan* (little scrap of paper).[9] As an illustration of saintly extravagance we can do no better than to quote the first three of these rules:

1. At every moment when a man is not engaged in the study of the Torah, especially at the time when he sits idly in his room or when he lies on his bed unable to fall asleep, he should reflect on the command to sanctify God's name (Leviticus 22:32) by suffering martyrdom. He should depict to himself that a huge and terrible fire, reaching to the skies, burns in front of him and he, for the sake of the sanctification of the Name, breaks his natural instinct and allows himself to be cast into the flames. God treats the intention as if it were the actual deed so that, far from sitting idle, he carries out a Divine command.

2. When he recites the first verse of the *Shema* (Deuteronomy 6:4) and the first of the eighteen benedictions of the Prayer, he should have the same thought in mind. He should also have in mind that if all the nations of the world were to torture him with every kind of severe torture to make him deny, Heaven forbid, God's unity, he will be prepared to endure all their tortures rather than admit that they are right, Heaven forbid. He should depict to himself that they actually do this to him and thereby he will have carried out his obligation, to recite the *Shema* and the Prayer, in the most fitting manner.

3. Also at the time of eating and drinking and during marital relations he should have the aforementioned intention in mind. Verbally as well as in his heart he should exclaim at once that he would have greater pleasure and enjoy it more when carrying out the precept of martyrdom in the aforesaid manner than any delight in the physical pleasure that derives from the leprous skin of the Serpent.[10] He should state, as proof that his pleasure in martyrdom would be greater, that, even if the murderers were to snatch him away in the middle of this meal or while he is engaged in sexual congress, he would take greater delight in fulfilling the precept of martyrdom than in the physical pleasure. However, he must take care really to mean it and have it fixed firmly in his mind. He must not fool himself and be, Heaven forbid, as one who tries to fool God.

HAYYIM HALBERSTAM OF ZANS

Of another hasidic master, R. Hayyim Halberstam of Zans (1793–1876), it is related that an ardent disciple, wishing to observe the conduct of the saint when he immersed himself in the *mikveh* at midnight, hid behind the benches so as not to be seen.[11] The awe-struck disciple watched as R. Hayyim, who suffered greatly from an affliction of the legs, wrenched off the plaster on his leg so that blood flowed from the wound. After undressing himself fully, except for his skullcap, the saint entered the *mikveh* and cried out in a strangled voice, "I accept upon myself the four death penalties of the Court!" He then called out "Stoning! Stoning!" many times and then continued, "Really to be stoned. I allow myself to be stoned to death for the sake of *En Sof*, blessed be He." After repeating this many times he immersed himself in the *mikveh*, breathing heavily as he pulled his head out of the water. He then raised his voice still higher, crying out, "Burning! Burning!" and then, "I allow myself to be burnt to death for the sake of the *En Sof*, blessed be He." He then immersed himself a second time. He repeated the process for the other two death penalties, slaying by the sword (here he drew his hand across his throat), and strangulation (here he seized his neck tightly in both hands as if to strangle himself). The poor disciple, witnessing in his imagination the master's death actually taking place, was moved to call out for the master to desist but managed to control himself. After all this, the saint quickly put on his clothes and called out to his retainer to escort him home, where he sat on the ground in mourning for the exile of the *Shekhinah (Tikkun Hatzot)*.

SOLOMON OF ZEHIL

The biography of the hasidic master R. Solomon of Zehil (1869–1945) includes a chapter, based on eyewitness accounts, on his saintly conduct.[12] This master was particularly noted for his ability to keep silent. He never spoke to others unless it was to give counsel or to reply to questions put to him. He once visited, together with his son, the Rebbe of Husiyatin. For about twenty minutes the two rebbes sat together without exchanging a single word. When they left, the son asked his father for his opinion of the Rebbe of Husiyatin. R. Solomon replied, "Did you not observe? He was on the boil like a hot kettle" [*er hat gekocht vie a kessel fier*]. R. Solomon would occasionally accept gifts of clothing from his followers, but he never bought any clothes for himself, preferring to go around in the shabbiest of rags. To objections that it was disgraceful for a scholar to be shabbily dressed, R. Solomon replied, "That is how I like it. Whoever does not like it let him do as he pleases." A little boy once noticed that R. Solomon liberally sprinkled salt into a dish he was about to eat, so as to make it less tasty. R. Solomon would not have done this so as to be observed by others; he did not realize that the little boy would notice. The rebbe's meals usually consisted of a few crusts left over from the poor boys for whom he provided free meals. Whether sitting in his house or walking on the street, this rebbe kept his head bowed at all times. When he was obliged to look at someone he would raise only his eyes, keeping his head bowed.

ARELE ROTH

The fiery hasidic master R. Arele Roth (1894–1944) compiled a huge volume, *Taharat ha-Kodesh,*[13] on the sin of seminal emissions, whether involuntarily or through masturbation.[13] He prescribes, as a penance for this and for other sins, various degrees of self-mortification. Among the penances mentioned are self-flagellation with a small strap but with all one's strength, with thirty-nine strokes on each hand and each leg daily, wearing sackcloth and ashes, rolling in the snow in the depth of winter, allowing oneself to be stung by insects, wandering in exile far from home, refraining from ever scratching an itch, and denying oneself sleep and tasty food.

SOLOMON SHAPIRA OF MUNKACS

The biographer of R. Solomon Shapira of Munkacs (1832–1893) relates that in his later years, this rebbe slept not in a bed but on a hard board, with a single pillow for his head and covered by a very thin blanket.[14] His grandson noticed that he would often leave his room during the night to remain in an unheated room in the depth of winter. He adds, "Goodness knows with what torments he afflicted himself in that cold, dark room, from which terrible screams were heard." He used to fast all day every Monday, and in certain periods of the year he used to fast for two or three days each week. When he was younger he did not fast, in order to reserve his strength for the study of the Torah and for prayer, but even in the hot summer months he would not touch a drop of water all day (although he would drink large quantities of water at night to prevent dehydration). For a period of eight years he had refrained from relations with his wife, with her permission (his parents had the same arrangement the generation before). He ate his main meal at night–plain bread with milk or coffee. After the meal he would walk to and fro in his room for a quarter of an hour, lost in *devekut;* then he would sit down to record his ideas. His biographer adds:

> In his later years he never smoked at all except on *Simhat Torah* towards the end of the day and on *Purim* and *Shushan Purim* he used to smoke a great deal and also at the meal in celebration of the completion of study of a talmudic tractate. On Hanukkah and at the meal following a circumcision he used to smoke a little. Often when he was in a state of severe depression he would smoke cigars so as to avoid a nervous breakdown [*nefilat ha-mohin*]. Also when he was on his travels he would smoke a great deal and they saw that this had some great significance, for he would never take a book with him to read nor would he engage in conversation (except just a little with his company of followers) but his thoughts were in great attachment (*devekut gadol*).

THE SAFED KABBALISTS

We have acounts of saintly extravagance in the Safed period–this, for instance, on Abraham Berukhim (1515–1593):[15]

> This pious one used to practice another custom. He would go out into the markets and the streets, calling for repentance. He would gather groups of penitents, lead them to the Ashkenazi synagogue, and say to them, "Do as you see me do." Then he would crawl into a sack, ordering them to drag him the entire length of the synagogue in order to mortify his flesh and humiliate his spirit. After this he enjoined them to

throw stones at him, each weighing a pound-and-a-half, which they would do.

In one of the rules of the Safed kabbalists, by Abraham Galante, we read:[16]

> On the eve of the New Moon all the people fast, including men, women, and students. And there is a place where they assemble on that day and remain the entire time, reciting penitential prayers, petitionary devotions, confession of sins, and practicing flagellation. And some among them place a large stone on their stomach in order to simulate the punishment of stoning. There are some individuals who "strangle" themselves with their hands and perform other things of a like nature. There are some persons who place themselves in a sack while others drag them around the synagogue.

All this certainly gives the lie to the notion that Judaism knows nothing of mortification of the flesh. Especially in the Middle Ages (witness the *Hasidey Ashkenaz* and others) the saints were not averse to practicing the most extreme mortifications. And they read these into the earlier period. Although the Talmud contains no record of such self-inflicted torments, the talmudic references in the Middle Ages to the third-century Amora R. Joseph's blindness were understood to mean that his sightlessness was self-inflicted. According to medieval legend, R. Joseph, unable to avoid looking outside himself, made himself blind.[17]

There is no reason to believe that the Jewish saints did not exhibit the same extreme behavior as their non-Jewish counterparts. As we have seen, they did.

5

THE SAINTLY IDEAL OF EQUANIMITY

In this chapter we will trace the saintly ideal of equanimity from its beginnings in Jewish thought to its appearance in Beshtian Hasidism, where it occupies a place of special prominence. The ideal variously called *equanimity, indifference,* or *disinterestedness* has its origin in Western thought, in the Stoic doctrine of *ataraxy,* the absence of passion.[1] This originally nonreligious ideal had an effect on the ascetic tendencies in early Christianity and, later, influenced the Sufi movement in Islam. Under the influence of Sufism,[2] the doctrine first appears in Bahya's *Duties of the Heart.*[3] This popular religious work was known, of course, to the hasidic masters, as it was to all devout Jews at the time when Hasidism arose in the eighteenth century. The ideal appealed particularly to the hasidic masters because it fits in with their typical doctrine of *bittul ha-yesh* (self-annihilation), with which it is often equated.[4] Moreover, Bahya attributes the doctrine to a *hasid,* in the context undoubtedly referring to a Sufi saint. Naturally, the latter-day hasidim were eager to live up to their name, probably believing that Bahya was referring to a Jewish *hasid.*

NEITHER PRAISE NOR DENIGRATE

In the passage in which this ideal occurs,[5] Bahya is describing ten principles by means of which believers can draw near to God's service free from the taint of self-interest. As the sixth of these principles, Bahya notes, "It should be the same to him [*shaveh etzlo* in the Hebrew translation from the original Arabic] whether people praise him or denigrate him."

Developing the same theme, Bahya writes:[6]

> They told of a certain saint (*hasid*) who asked one of his companions, "Have you attained equanimity [*hanishtavita*]?"
>
> The companion replied, "In what sense?"
>
> The saint asked, "Are praise and denigration all the same to you?"
>
> "No," said he.
>
> "In that case," the saint retorted, "you have not yet attained it. Make an effort and you may yet succeed in attaining this stage, the loftiest stage among the saints [*ha-hasidim*] and the ultimate of all delightful traits."

The doctrine as well as the story of the saint appears, without reference to Bahya, in a slightly different version in *Sefer Meirat Eynayim,* by the kabbalist Isaac of Acre (late thirteenth to fourteenth century).[7][8] This author writes:

> Whoever attains to the secret of attachment (*ha-hitdabbekut*) will attain to the secret of equanimity (*ha-hishtavut*) and will attain to the secret of solitude (*ha-hitbodedut*). Once he has attained to the secret of solitude he will attain to the gift of the holy spirit (*ruah ha-kodesh*) and then to prophecy, so that he will be able to foretell the future. The secret of equanimity was imparted to me by Rabbi Abner.[9] A certain sage came to one of the hermits (*ha-mitbodedim*) requesting to be admitted into their fraternity. The hermit said to him, "My son, it is clear to God that your motives are worthy, but tell me this, have you attained to equanimity?"
>
> He replied, "Master, please explain what you mean."

> Said he, "Supposing there are two men, one of whom pays you honors, while the other insults you. Are they both the same in your eyes?"
>
> The sage replied, "No master. When honors are paid to me I am pleased and experience a sense of bliss, but when I am insulted I feel aggrieved, although I have no wish to take revenge or to hate the one who has insulted me."
>
> "Go in peace, my son," said the hermit. "For as long as you have not attained to equanimity, to the extent that insults to your person leave you totally unaffected, you are not ready for your thoughts to be bound to the One on high that you may be admitted into membership of our fraternity. However, go away and humble yourself still more in true humility until you do attain to equanimity and then you will be able to become a hermit."
>
> The significance of equanimity is that it brings about attachment to God in thought. For when the mind is attached and joined to God, a man has no awareness of anything due to him and pays no heed to "diviners and magicians" (Deuteronomy 18:10).

The hasidic masters did not know of Isaac of Acre's work; it had not been published in their day. However, they did know the work *Reshit Hokhmah,* by the Safed kabbalist Elijah de Vidas, who quotes, in a slightly different version, the beginning of the Isaac of Acre passage on the virtue of solitude.[10] It is just possible that the early hasidic masters had an oral tradition in which Isaac's teachings circulated, although they do not refer to this anywhere in their writings. They also had access to another source in which the ideal of equanimity is mentioned in passing. This is the work by another famed Safed kabbalist, Hayyim Vital, entitled *Shaarey Kedushah.* Vital writes:[11]

> He should take care to avoid every unworthy trait, for these make the essential soul filthy, especially the sin of pride. This he should avoid to the extent that he considers himself to be like the threshold upon which all tread. Humility (*shiflut*)[12] should become so much part of his nature [lit. "the heart"] that he experiences no joy from honors paid to him and no distress from insults, and the two should be the same (*shaveh*) in his eyes.

In the school of the Maggid of Mesirech, disciple of the Baal Shem Tov, founder of the hasidic movement,[13] the doctrine of equanimity is read into the verse "I have set the Lord always before me" (Psalms 16:8). The Hebrew for "I have set" is *shiviti,* which, by a play on the word, is rendered as "I have equanimity" (*hishtavut*). Thus the Maggid comments:[14]

> *I have set the Lord always before me; shiviti* denotes equanimity. Whatsoever befalls a man, it should be all the same to him, whether people praise him or despise him.[15] And so, too, with regard to all other matters. And so, too, with regard to eating; whether he eats delicacies or other food, it should be all the same to him since his evil inclination has gone entirely from him. Whatever befalls him he should say "Behold, this is from God and if it is good in His eyes, so be it," but his intention should be for the sake of Heaven so that in essence there is no difference. This is a most elevated stage.

The Maggid, like the majority of the hasidic masters, does not actually praise the solely ascetic way, despite the ascetic tendencies in his thought. The obligation to rescue the "holy sparks,"[16] on which Hasidism sets such great store, demands that the *hasid* be engaged in the world. But, the Maggid states, he should eat and drink whatever comes to hand without thought of his own pleasure. If it happens to be good and tasty food, then he should see that as the will of God, but he should have in mind that he eats the food solely because God evidently wishes him so to do. The Maggid goes on to say that "in essence" (i.e., in his innermost being), it should be all the same to him whether God wishes him to enjoy good food or less-than-wholesome food. The Maggid has here extended the ideal of equanimity beyond Bahya's indifference to praise and blame. For the Maggid, the ideal has come to denote total indifference to all wordly matters.

In a work attributed to another early hasidic master, Menahem Mendel of Premyslani (b. 1728), there is a further elaboration of the doctrine,[17] probably deriving from a degree of sensitivity to the taunts of the *mitnaggedim* that the *hasidim,* in their pursuit of piety, neglected the study of the Torah. Menahem Mendel writes:

> The Baal Shem Tov laid down a great principle, that of equanimity (*ha-hishtavut*). This means that it should be all the same to a man whether

> people imagine him to be an ignoramus or one who knows the whole of the Torah. Such an attitude brings about attachment (*devekut*) to God all the time. So absorbed is he in this attachment that he has no time to think of such matters, for he is engaged in attaching himself to God, blessed be He.

In this version of the doctrine it would seem that equanimity is advocated as a means to attachment (*devekut*)–the opposite of Isaac of Acre's scheme, in which it is *devekut* that leads to equanimity. The text is probably corrupt, however, since Menahem Mendel himself goes on to say that as a result of *devekut* there is no time to think of self.[18]

DISDAIN FOR PRAISE

Jacob Isaac, the Seer of Lublin (d. 1815), disciple of the Maggid, analyzed the ideal of equanimity in the following story, told by Moses of Sambur, his disciple.[19] A man was heard to say, in the presence of the seer, that he violently disliked it when people praised him. Upon hearing this, the seer shook his head as if in protest. "From this I understood," remarked Moses of Sambur, "that the ideal of equanimity, referred to in *The Duties of the Heart* in the name of the saint, does not mean that it should be as unpleasant to a man when he is praised as it is when he is denigrated. Rather, the ideal means that he should be in his own eyes as if he were nothing at all, so that whether he is praised or denigrated he remains totally unaffected by it all, as if it were all said of a piece of wood or a stone. That is the true ideal of equanimity."

The ideal persisted among the later hasidic masters. Dov Baer of Liovo (1827–1876), a master who for a time rebelled against the movement, is reported as having taught this ideal.[20] Dov Baer referred to his father, Israel of Ruzhyn (1797–1850), great-grandson of the Maggid, as one who truly practiced equanimity:

> Abraham, our father, said, *I am but dust and ashes* (Genesis 18:27). It is indeed an excellent application of humility when a man thinks no more of himself than the dust of the earth, than which there is nothing lower. Yet when a man sows in earth, that which is sown grows there. So, too, for such a man; it is still possible for him to be affected when something

> grows for him. But (based on *Hullin* 89a) Moses said, *And we are nothing* (Exodus 16:8), and from nothing, nothing grows. For such a man, everything that befalls him is the same. Whether he is given fame and honor or their opposite, he remains totally unaffected. My father, on whom be peace, remained totally unaffected by anything in the whole wide world, except on one occasion when he was very young in years. Yet, if the earlier saints were like angels, we are only human beings.

It is fascinating to note how the original Stoic ideal, which became a religious ideal of great merit in Christian asceticism and later among the Sufis, was adopted by Bahya and other Jewish teachers in the Middle Ages until it found its expression in the new mystical movement of Hasidism.

6

SAINTLY RAPTURES

Apart from legends, there are very few accounts in the literature of Jewish saintliness of even second-hand reports of the kind of saintly experience known in Christian mystical theology as *rapture* or *ecstasy* or *mystical trance.* We will note some of these accounts in this chapter. The terms used in the literature for the kind of experience we are considering, in which the saint transcends normal consciousness to meet God directly, are *aliyat neshamah* (ascent of the soul) or *hitpashtut ha-gashmiyut* (the stripping off of corporeality). In my book *Jewish Mystical Testimonies,* I quoted a number of such accounts. Moshe Idel has recently studied in detail the most comprehensive example of direct mystical experience, the prophetic kabbalism of Abraham Abulafia (thirteenth century).[1] This mystic, whose work was almost totally ignored until the last century, provides not only accounts of the experience but techniques for its attainment, including breathing exercises and the use of music.[2] There is now presented some further material on the subject. Of course, the greatest caution must be exercised in this area in distinguishing between pious legend and what purports to be a real account of the experience, at first or second hand, without considering whether the experience actually took place or how it is to be explained psychologically and theologically. It is the phenomenon of saintly rapture that is our concern in this chapter. One thing is certain: The belief has persisted throughout that the saint can at times enjoy the intimate, transcendent awareness of the reality of God in a way that renders his physical faculties dormant so that he is lost in rapture. Under the heading "Fullness of God," Van Der Leeuw describes the experience: "The enthusiast then, in the full sense of this word, knows that he is being swept away by some overruling power which lifts him completely out of himself and fills him with new insight, new strength, new life."[3]

PHINEHAS OF KORETZ

The early hasidic master R. Phinehas of Koretz said:[4]

> At the time when the Torah was given, the souls of Israel departed from their bodies (*Shabbat* 88b), for otherwise they would have been incapable of receiving the Torah. Only when their souls were embraced by that awe and dread when they heard the Decalogue, did they then receive the Torah. But our teacher, Moses, the most humble of men, who thought nothing of himself, his soul did not retreat in dread and his soul did not depart from his body but remained where it had been. He was in the category of the stripping off of one form to be clothed by another, since he was as nothing in himself.

He continued:

> The world imagines that the stripping off of corporeality is a marvel, but that is incorrect. It is only that when a man is as nothing to the utmost degree in his own eyes, he is in the category of stripping off the form, and then the ascent of soul comes automatically.

Thus, for R. Phinehas, once the self has been completely transcended, the soul ascends to God of its own accord. It is not a marvel or a miracle but entirely "natural" for such a saint.

DOV BAER OF LUBAVITCH

The second rebbe of the *Habad* movement in Hasidism, R. Dov Baer of Lubavitch (1773–1827), was believed to have experienced regular mystical trances. For instance, Jacob of Kaidenow reports the following, told to him by another *hasid:*[5]

> Immediately after we had eaten our meal, the retainer came to me in great haste, saying, "If you wish to gaze at the face of our master and teacher, now is the time." I replied that I had no wish to do so because I knew that the rebbe, in his humility, is very much opposed to people gazing at him. The retainer said, "I swear to you that now he will not notice that you are there," so I said to myself that it was worthwhile to observe this phenomenon. I went along with the retainer, who opened the door of the rebbe's sanctum. Lo and behold, what did I see but the holy master standing immobile in the middle of the room without any apparent vitality, his face burning like flames of flashing torches and his eyes open. I said to myself, he is bound to have seen me and be annoyed with me, and I retreated. But the retainer seized hold of my coat and shouted out, "Have no fear at all, for now he is in the upper worlds, even though you see his body in this world."
>
> I said, "How do you know these things, since you are only a common person?"
>
> But he replied, "It is not due to my grasp of any mysteries but from experience. For not once or twice but many times have I observed it of his holiness." So I gazed at his holy face and became myself aware that he neither sees nor hears, even though his eyes are open, and his bodily instincts are completely dormant. So there I stood by the door, gazing with the utmost perception at his holy face, perchance to witness some vital movement, however slight. But only his eyes were open and his face burned like the Seraphim. I remained there from ten o'clock until three, the retainer, meanwhile, going in and out, and his holiness standing there like a brand plucked from the fire, immobile and without any sensation. . . . At three o'clock the retainer said to my coachman, "Set the table, for it is time to have something to eat, for he has not eaten all day." He set the table and they made ready a vessel for the rebbe to wash his hands, appreciating that although the rebbe's eyes were open, he did not see what was going on. The retainer then said, "Why not

wake up his holiness to wash his hands because he has not eaten all day?" The coachman replied that he was afraid to try to wake him up, so the retainer said that, in that case, he must do it. The retainer then went up to his holiness, took hold of the sleeve of his coat, and said, "Please, your holiness, wash your hands." He made no reply but simply moved to the middle of the room, where he stood as before. Since he now had his face to the wall, I said to myself, there is nothing more to see of this wondrous sight. So I left for my room. The next day the retainer said, "I shall tell you about the wondrous sight you saw last night. After you had left the room, his holiness continued to stand there with his face to the wall until four o'clock and then he went of his own accord to the table, eating the meal with a joyfulness I had never before witnessed. I said, 'Master, perhaps I shall be privileged that you tell me the reason for such joy, greater than any I have witnessed since I have known your honor.' He replied, 'Why so surprised? I have never, in fact, experienced such joy. For whenever I expound the teachings in public, our father and master, his soul is in Eden, is wont to reveal himself to me in the middle of the exposition, whereas the last time he revealed himself to me right at the beginning. And I also saw the Baal Shem Tov and his disciple, the Maggid of Mesirech, and after the exposition they departed, leaving behind only my father, who said to me that the Baal Shem Tov and the Maggid praised my exposition and requested that I continue to expound in the same manner in the future. The reason I stood in the middle of the room is that I repeated the exposition to my father and he, in turn, revealed to me new secrets. From these, higher than the human mind can grasp, I have this great joy.' " Now from this true story the reader will understand something of the rebbe's most exalted stage. . . .

MEIR OF APTA

A similar account is found in a work on the life and marvels of R. Jacob Isaac of Pshycha (1766–1814), known as "the Holy Jew."[6] R. Meir of Apta, disciple of this master, related to his disciples that once, on a visit to the master, he was warned by the latter of the spiritual risks encountered in attaining elevated stages (*madregot*).[7] Soon after, said R. Meir, he experienced such high elevation, but it was taken from him. Nevertheless, he said, one thing remained. The tale continues:

> He [R. Meir] told his disciples that they should observe and learn this one stage (*madregah*) from him, for it is good and advantageous to the soul. This is, that he would send his soul to immerse itself in the River Dinur (on high) so that on its return to the body it will be incomparably pure, shining, and polished. No sooner had he spoken thus than his head fell to the arm of his chair and he fainted without seeming to have retained any vestige of life. Had they not heard what he had said, their hearts would have stopped in terror and they would have thought that he had actually died. He remained in that state for a time, and then his soul gradually returned. He began to breathe and he reverted to his former strength, and they sighed with relief. He said to them, "I cannot begin to describe to you the great delight, the pleasant nearness, the sweet beauty and the purity and polish of the soul that has enjoyed such an experience."

Soresky remarks that the hasidim relate the story of another disciple of R. Meir who had witnessed Meir's trance state and who, after he had retold the tale to his disciples, himself went into this mystical trance:[8]

> After a time, the rebbe, R. Leibush, of blessed memory, had his own company of *hasidim,* and a group of his elite God-seekers surrounded him. One day he began to tell them the details of the ascent (of R. Meir) as if it were then taking place. When he reached the end of the tale, which he told with great feeling, how he had witnessed R. Meir's soul ascend, he, too, attained suddenly an actual stripping off of corporeality (*hitpashtut ha-gashmiyut*) that seemed to approximate death, and the holy disciples saw it for themselves.[9]

HAYYIM HALBERSTAM OF ZANS

There are numerous tales of the saints going into trances in order to become impervious to pain. There is, for instance, the story of R. Hayyim Halberstam of Zans, who refused anesthesia during a major operation on his leg. He claimed to have a tradition from his teacher, R. Naftali of Ropshitz, about a certain *yihud* (unification), the delight in which brings about a state so transcendental that the one who practices it is oblivious to pain at the time. The surgeon who performed the operation believed that R. Hayyim had died under the knife. But gradually the saint began to breathe, and he emerged safely from his self-induced trance.[10]

MORDECAI SHARABI

Among Oriental Jews, too, there are many tales of the saints falling into a mystical trance. In Rafaeli's biography of the contemporary Yemenite mystic R. Mordecai Sharabi, the following is related:[11]

> This was told to the writer of these lines by a number of people who were present when it happened. Once, during the third meal on the Sabbath, while a large number of people were seated around the table of the saint (*ha-tzaddik*), our master closed his eyes in slumber. When they saw that the saint was asleep at the table, they stopped their singing. The saint's wife entered the room with a plate containing slices of melon. When she saw the strange sight she called out to him, "Abba! Abba! I have brought you some melon." Suddenly our master opened his eyes, and those present witnessed an awesome sight. The eyes of the saint were glowing as red as scarlet, with two great rays proceeding from them. Dread and terror fell upon those present and none dared to ask the master why his eyes were glowing.

ZECHARIAH MENDEL OF YAROSLAV

Some of the maxims of R. Zechariah Mendel of Yaroslav, disciple of R. Elimelech of Lizensk, are relevant here. R. Zechariah Mendel states that when a man carries out a *mitzvah* or when he offers his prayers, his sole intention should be to give satisfaction (*nahat ruah*) to God.[12] If, for instance, he finds it difficult to concentrate while praying, he should be much grieved, not because he is himself displeased, but rather because his inability to concentrate prevents him from giving God that which is due to Him. On the numinous fear of God, Zechariah Mendel writes:[13]

> When a man attains to great and powerful fear of God, so that he seems about to die as a result of the dread he experiences, he should take care to

> bear it in his faith that God will give him strength to withstand it. He should not pray to God to take this fear from him, and if he really does expire in the process, happy is he and happy his portion that he has suffered such a death.

What a way to go! Hasidic legend has it that R. Elimelech would place his watch on the desk in front of him when he began to pray in order to be reminded not to lose himself in the world of eternity and to return to the world of time.

R. Zechariah Mendel does not advocate only worship in fear, however. Joy must also be present. Thus he observes:[14]

> A man may offer his prayers in fear and without joy because he is afflicted with melancholia. Another may offer his prayers with joy and without fear because his sanguinity has gotten the better of him. The worthy attitude is that in which both love and fear are combined. It also belongs to the main idea of fear that it should come from Heaven, not that he should awaken fear in himself, for that is in the category of female waters [a kabbalistic expression for the impulse which comes from below]. At times a man is worthy for fear to descend upon him and his mind becomes refined so that his tears flow of their own accord as a result of the dread he experiences.

Joy without fear, remarks Zechariah Mendel,[15] is no more than a mere superficiality. He believes that it is possible for a man to be given a message from on high:[16]

> Occasionally, a man is worthy for there to be imparted to him some information from Heaven. This happens when, as soon as he awakes from his sleep, a verse falls into his mind. He should then reflect on that verse and he will see that they are offering him some rebuke, contained in that verse, or are showing him something he should observe. This is a tremendous idea.

THE CONCEPT OF DEVEKUT

Gershom Scholem has analyzed the concept of *devekut* with special reference to its role in Hasidism.[17] As in some of the examples we have quoted, *devekut,* "attachment to God," often denotes ecstasy, rapture, self-transcendence, mystic trance. Scholem rightly sees the source of the whole concept in Nahmanides' comment on "To love the Lord thy God, to walk in all His ways and to cleave unto Him" (Deuteronomy 11:12). Nahmanides says that it is plausible to suggest that the word *cleave (devekut)* in the verse refers to having God always in the mind, even when engaged in worldly matters.[18] It is further plausible to suggest, he adds, that those who have attained this state partake of eternal life even in this earthly life because they have made themselves an abode for the *Shekhinah.* According to Scholem, the novelty of the Baal Shem Tov's theology lies in the fact that *devekut* can be attained not only *in spite of* engagement in the world but *because* of it. This is certainly correct, as Scholem's illustrations demonstrate. But the aspect of *devekut* that is the subject of this chapter, the rapturous flight of the soul to God, is a separate and intimate factor, especially in the life of prayer.

Leaving aside, then, the particular hasidic emphasis, dealt with comprehensively in Scholem's essay, we can note these two descriptions of the saintly life in which this feature appears, both quoted by Scholem. In Scholem's translation,[19] the passage in Azikri's *Sefer Haredim*[20] states that the early saints (*Hasidim ha-Rishonim*) would spend nine hours a day in prayer "for the spiritual activities of retreat and *devekut.*" He continues:

> [T]hey used to imagine the light of the *Shekhinah* above their heads, as though it were flowing all around them and they were sitting in the midst of the light, and thus have I found it explained in an old manuscript of the ancient ascetics.[21] And while in that state they are all trembling as a natural effect, but rejoicing in trembling.

THE POWER OF HOLINESS

The other extra-hasidic source is Luzzatto's account of his final stages on the path of holiness.[22] Luzzatto states that holiness (*kedushah*) is essentially a divine gift, but man must prepare himself for the gift by keeping aloof from whatever is grossly material, and by clinging at all times to that which is godly. It is only when God then imparts to man some of His holiness that man is rendered holy. That is why the rabbis say that the Patriarchs are the *Merkavah* (the divine chariot).[23] If, after passing through all the stages mapped out in Luzzatto's *Mesillat Yesharim* a man cleaves to God with an ardent love and profound awe by reason of his comprehending God's greatness and majesty, he will gradually break away from all that is physical.

> In all his doings he will succeed in centering the mind upon the mystery of true communion, until there is poured out upon him a spirit from on high, and the name of the Creator, blessed be He, will abide within him as it does within all holy beings. He will then literally become an angel of the Lord. With the help of God his soul will become strong and will be able to conquer all corporeal desires. It will cleave to the holiness of God, blessed be He, and thus be rendered perfect. Thence it will rise to still greater heights, and will be endowed with the holy spirit. Then will his power of comprehension exceed mortal limitations. In his communion with God he will attain such excellence that he will be entrusted with the power of resurrection, as were Elijah and Elisha.

THE RAPTURE OF DEATH

There is a remarkable passage on the subject of saintly raptures in Hayyim Attar's *Or ha-Hayyim.*[24] Attar is commenting on the verse "after the death of the two sons of Aaron, when they drew near before the Lord, and died" (Leviticus 16:1). He first observes that the two sons, like all the other saints (*tzaddikim*), died by a divine kiss; the only difference was that for the other saints, the "kiss" drew near to them, whereas the two sons of Aaron drew near to the kiss. The verse "they drew near before the Lord, and they died" means that these saints did not cease from drawing nearer to the sweet, delightful longing of their attachment (*devekut*) to God, even though they knew that they would expire in longing as a result. Such a state, Attar continues, is inconceivable to the human mind and unintelligible to anyone who would try to record it. The experience is beyond comparison.

There is a natural recoil from the experience when it presents itself. The saint is torn between his longing and his natural instinct to resist its death-inviting allure, and he struggles against this compelling force. This is why the prophets are sometimes described as insane.[25] Once this experience has taken hold of the saint's innermost being, he comes to abhor his flesh and he leaves it behind, his soul returning to the Source.

After this introduction, Attar makes the following cryptic comment, long a puzzle to his readers:

> I shall explain to whoever reflects on the innermost comprehension of that which is comprehended (*haskalat ha-muskal*) that the comprehension of that which is comprehended does involve comprehension, but when it is comprehended the one who comprehends comprehends that the object of his comprehension cannot be comprehended. When he comprehends of his own accord, and yet it is not of himself, he then comprehends that that which is comprehended is so comprehended from a source that cannot be comprehended by the intelligence and it is conveyed to those who comprehend by their becoming united with this comprehension, in accord with the mystery of a soul added to a soul. At this stage, all human comprehension becomes superfluous, like the king's crown and throne in relation to the king himself. The one who has reached this stage will sense that there is a life above life, concerning which Moses said "choose life" (Deuteronomy 30:19), the ultimate destiny, not that which is generally understood as such. And he will bless the living God who has given this treasure to His chosen people.

Reuben Margaliot lists authors who have tried their hand at deciphering Attar's riddle.[26] Margaliot himself suggests the following explanation of the cryptic passage: Whoever reflects on the way in which the comprehension of the truth (about God) is attained will come to appreciate that whatever the human mind can grasp of this tremendous topic is no more than preparation and cannot be considered to be in any way a true comprehension, since that is beyond the capacity of the human mind. The true comprehension comes from God in His goodness, in a way that is beyond the human mind's ability to grasp. It is God's grace, which pours out on those who prepare themselves to receive it, that endows them with an extra soul, a soul added to their original soul. At this stage the saint will become aware that all human comprehension is as inessential as the crown and throne of the king in relation to the king himself. The spiritual delight attained through such comprehension constitutes living at its highest. It is the very life of life.

Attar returns to the theme of rapture-induced death in his comment on the verse "My soul failed me when he spoke" (Song of Songs 5:6):[27] "The soul departs from the body without the departure being felt, so great is the delight that is experienced." On the verse "And these words, which I command thee this day, shall be upon thy heart" (Deuteronomy 6:6), Attar writes:[28]

> The verse wishes to teach the children of Israel the method by which to attain to the love of God. For love is not an act where a man can force his heart to do the will of the king but is a matter of the heart. For as long as his heart lacks any sense of that which produces yearning, a man has no love, even if he tries to coerce the heart with every kind of coercion. Consequently, this counsel is given by God, who gives counsel: "These words shall be *upon* thy heart." That is to say, if he constantly takes the words to heart there will be born in the heart powerful longing and desire for spirituality, and the heart will race to love God in all that He commands. And we, too, orphans of orphans though we are, sense it. For greater is the desire of our heart and longing for the Creator more than all the riches of the world and regal honors. And every pleasant thing is sensed as loathsome and despicable in comparison with the smallest portion of that which we comprehend through the sensation of having the words in our heart. Happy are we. How goodly is our portion. I have referred to this idea in many places.

THE EROTIC ELEMENT

Scholem, in his chapter on the *Hasidey Ashkenaz,* has called attention to the erotic element in the mysticism of this group.[29] As in Christian mysticism, there is no doubt that this element is often present in the literature of Jewish saintliness; the raptures of the saints have been compared to the intense experiences of sexual love. Eleazar of Worms, leader of the *Hasidey Ashkenaz* movement, wrote, as we noted earlier, a work called *Sodey Razayya* (Secret Mysteries), a part of which found its way into the curious book *Sefer Raziel.* This book purports to be a series of communications to Adam, after the Fall, from the angel Raziel. Here Raziel instructs Adam on the love of God:[30]

> The root of love is to love the Lord. The soul is filled with love, bound in great joy in the bonds of love. Such joy chases away from the heart all bodily pleasures and worldly delights. The powerful joy of love seizes hold of his heart so that he thinks all the time, How can I do the will of God? . . . The love of Heaven in his heart is like the flame attached to the coal. He does not gaze at women, he does not engage in frivolous talk, but he concerns himself only with doing God's will, and he sings songs in order to be filled with joy in his love of God.[31]

The truth is that the erotic element is found even in Maimonides' description of the love of God:[32]

> What is the fitting love of God? It is that a man should love God with an extraordinary powerful love to the extent that his soul becomes tied to the love of God so that he pines for it unceasingly. It should be as if he were lovesick, unable to get the woman he loves out of his mind, pining for her all the time when he eats or drinks. Even more than this should be the love of God in the hearts of those who love Him and yearn constantly for Him, as He has commanded us, "with all your heart and with all your soul" (Deuteronomy 6:5). Solomon expresses it in the form of a parable: "For I am lovesick" (Song of Songs 2:5). The whole of the Song of Songs is, in fact, a parable to illustrate this theme.

Elijah de Vidas devotes no fewer than twelve chapters in his *Reshit Hokhmah* to the theme of the love of God. Here he tells the story, in the name of Isaac of Acre, of the man who once fell hopelessly in love with a princess and, out of unrequited love, gave up the world to become a hermit. Isaac of Acre draws the conclusion that the love of God does not come from nowhere, but derives from the sublimation of natural love.

Hayyim Attar, in discussing the meaning of loving God with *all* the heart, writes:[33]

> This means that a man should strive to bring the love of God into his heart and to be on fire with that love to the utmost extent of the heart's capacity. That is why it is said "with *all* thy heart." For the heart of a man has a desire for any woman but more so for a pretty woman and more so still for a very beautiful woman and most of all for a woman without peer. Scripture demands that the love of God be carved in the heart to the utmost degree.

7

SAINTLY CONDUCT

The closest one comes to a set of monastic rules in Judaism, which knows nothing of monasticism as such, is the rules drawn up by the Jewish saints for themselves, whether as members of a fraternity, as in sixteenth-century Safed, or as individuals. These rules are usually termed *hanhagot* (procedures, ways of conducting oneself). In addition, the hagiographical works often describe the saintly hero's life in terms of the rules he followed, his detailed procedures in the conduct of his holy life. The former type of material is more reliable. In the second-hand material, pious biographers are motivated by veneration and are consequently not averse to conscious exaggeration, either by inventing practices they believe that the saint might have adopted or by elevating casual observance at a given time and place into modes of behavior followed unfailingly.

A further example of the genre is the ethical will, a compilation of which was published by Israel Abrahams with the title *Hebrew Ethical Wills.* Both Abrahams and Gries, the great pioneers in the study of the *hanhagot* literature,[1] have called attention to the popularity of much of this kind of material, and in this they are undoubtedly correct. But our concern in this chapter is with the elitist aspects of the genre, in which the rules are intended not for the ordinary pious Jew, but for those eager to impose upon themselves, and upon fellow travelers on the saintly path, a far more severe regimen. It is usually possible to distinguish the saintly rules from more generally applicable counsel by examining the context in which they occur.

SAINTLY RULES FROM THE GEONIM

The earliest document containing saintly rules is found in the Geonic collection of Responsa (dating from not later than the tenth century) known as *Shaarey Teshuvah.* This collection was first published in Salonika in 1702. A critical edition was published (Leipzig 1858) by Y. F. Halevi. The hasidic master, R. Gershon Henoch Leiner of Radzhyn (1839–1891), published these rules with a commentary at the end of his *Sefer Orhot Hayyim.*[2] The Responsum in *Shaarey Teshuvah* in which the rules are recorded is number 178.[3] They are headed "These are the saintly rules (*miley de-hasiduta*) that were followed by Rav but, after him, those who obeyed him were unable to hold fast to them so that each held fast to (only) one of them." Rav is the famous third-century Babylonian teacher; "those who obeyed him" are his disciples and later teachers. The author of the Responsum, probably in reply to a questioner (though this is not stated explicitly), attributes these rules to Rav without giving his source for either this attribution or the conduct of the disciples. But it is clear that his "tradition" is based on talmudic passages.

The following are the ten rules as found in the Responsum, together with the possible talmudic sources as supplied by R. Leiner.

1. He never walked four cubits with upright posture [based on *Berakhot* 43b, but no mention there of Rav]. His disciple R. Judah followed him in this. [R. Leiner suggests that the author of the Responsum had the reading in *Kiddushin* 31a, "R. Judah never walked four cubits with upright posture," and finds this reading in Abraham b. Nathan of Lunel's *Sefer ha-Manhig.*][4]

2. He never walked four cubits with uncovered head. And R. Huna followed him in this. [This is evidently based on *Kiddushin* 31a,

but there the R. Huna referred to is R. Huna son of R. Joshua, not the R. Huna who was Rav's disciple. See *Kiddushin* 29b that R. Huna was annoyed with R. Hamnuna because the latter was not wearing a turban.]

3. All his days Rav ate three meals on the Sabbath. And R. Nahman followed him in this. [See *Shabbat* 118b.]

4 and 5. [So in our texts of the Responsum]. Rav never gazed on either side and not even in front of him. We know this because Rav said (*Menahot* 29a, 110a; *Berakhot* 43b; *Niddah* 24a), "Are you Simi?" which shows that he did not look at him and did not know to whom he was speaking until he heard his voice. And R. Joseph and R. Sheshet followed him in this but were unable to keep to it, so they blinded themselves. [Evidently, the text counts these as two rules–(4) Rav did not gaze on either side, and (5) Rav did not even look in front of him. But R. Leiner is no doubt correct that this is a copyist's error and that these two are a single item, number 4, number 5 having been lost and incorrectly supplied by the copyist. The reference to R. Joseph and R. Sheshet is based on the talmudic descriptions of these two teachers as being blind, and there is a legend, to which the Responsum evidently alludes, that R. Joseph voluntarily made himself blind.[5] R. Leiner quotes Maimonides (*Yad, Deot* 2:5), who attributes to Rav the quality that he never engaged in idle chatter. Leiner surmises that this is the original rule number 5 of the Responsum. He may well be right, but one might question whether he ought to have recorded this in his text of the Responsum as if it were certain, particularly since the wording is Maimonides'.]

6. When Rav would go to the house of study he would enter in a roundabout way and would avoid passing by the scholars so as not to bother the congregation [who would have had to rise in respect when he passed.] And R. Zera and Abbaye followed him in this. [The statement about Rav is based on *Megillah* 22b. The statement about R. Zera and Abbaye is in *Kiddushin* 33a.]

7. Rav never ate at an optional banquet [as opposed to a religious celebration] because of his fear that the food served may have contained tallow, blood, or the sinew of the thigh. [The source is obviously *Hullin* 95b, but there is no mention there of Rav's fear of eating forbidden food. R. Leiner believes this addition to be a copyist's error, the original

text simply stating that Rav never ate at a banquet unless it was a religious celebration.]

8. Whenever someone offended Rav, he would be the first to go to make it up to him. And Rav Zutra, son of R. Nahman, followed him in this. [The source for Rav is *Yoma* 87a. The source for "Mar Zutra" is *Megillah* 28a, although, in our texts, not "son of R. Nahman."]

9. Rav was always careful to wear *tefillin,* and R. Sheshet followed him in this. [R. Leiner refers to Maimonides' quote in this vein [*Yad, Tefillin* 4:25] that Rav never walked four cubits without *tefillin.* For R. Sheshet the source is *Shabbat* 118b.]

10. Rav had a pleasant voice, and it was his custom to lead the services and to be a transmitter of his master's teachings (*meturgeman*) and for whoever required his services, in order to fulfill the verse "Honor the Lord with thy substance" (Proverbs 3:9). And R. Hiyya bar Abba followed him in this, as it is stated, "R. Hiyya bar Abba, son of Bar Kappara's sister, had a pleasant voice and when he led the congregation in prayer, he would say, 'Please the Lord with that which He has been pleased to give you.' Therefore the verse says 'Honor the Lord with your substance.'" [The source for Rav leading the congregation in prayer may be, R. Leiner notes, *Megillah* 22a. The quote about R. Hiyya bar Abba would seem to be from the Jerusalem Talmud *Berakhot* 2:8.]

The practice of anthologizing talmudic passages for the purpose of providing saintly rules was continued in the moralistic literature. This literature was also intended for the ordinary pietist but often contains saintly rules, anthologized, as in the Geonic Responsum, from casual references in the Talmud. Once the Talmud had become accepted as a sacred work second only to the Bible, accounts of saintly conduct found in the Talmud came to be viewed as a set of divine instructions for saintly living.

SAFED RULES

In his essay on the mystics of Safed, Solomon Schechter published from manuscript the *hanhagot* of two leaders of the Safed circle, Moses Cordovero and Abraham Galante.[6] Lawrence Fine has studied the background to these and similar *hanhagot* and has supplied an introduction and learned notes.[7] Clearly, these rules were for saintly mystics, and their purpose was to assist the flow of divine grace throughout all Creation, on the basis of the kabbalistic doctrine that humankind, created in God's image, had been given the power to influence the upper world of the *Sefirot* by virtuous deeds. By obeying these rules, the saint sends powerfully beneficent impulses, which promote harmony in the upper realms so that the divine sustaining energy can function more effectively.

In Fine's translation, the *hanhagot* of Abraham Galante begin:

> Holy and worthy customs practiced in the land of Israel which were copied from a manuscript written by the perfect and righteous sage, our honored Rabbi and teacher, Abraham Galante, a resident of Safed, may it be rebuilt and established speedily in our day.

There follows the list of rules, of which this is a representative sampling:

> There are the rules "which if a man practices, he shall live by them" (Leviticus 18:5).
>
> 6. On the seventh night of Passover they rise at midnight and read the "Song of the Sea" in *Midrash va-Yosha;* they sing songs of Torah until dawn. They then recite petitionary prayers, at the conclusion of which they rise to their feet to sing the psalm "When Israel went out of Egypt" (Psalm 114) in a sweet voice.
>
> 9. Every Sabbath eve they go out into the field or the courtyard of the synagogue to welcome the Sabbath. Everyone dresses in his Sabbath clothes. They recite the psalm "Give thanks to the Lord, O heavenly beings" (Psalm 29) and the Sabbath hymn, followed by the "Psalm for the Sabbath" (Psalm 92).
>
> 27. There are certain especially pious individuals who fulfill the tithe obligation [to the poor] by doubling it, that is, with one fifth of all their earnings. They set aside their money in a chest so that they have it available to them and can give generously in fulfillment of their pledge. Even among the poor themselves there are those who follow this custom.

Cordovero's *hanhagot* begin:[8]

> These are the rules which the saintly Rabbi Moshe Cordovero, may his memory be for an everlasting blessing, taught "which if a man practices, he shall live by them" [Leviticus 18:15, evidently the standard opening of *hanhagot*].

Following are six of Cordovero's thirty-six rules:

> 1. One should avoid anger altogether, because anger leads a person to commit a variety of transgressions.
>
> 2. Let an individual always enjoy the company of others and behave towards them with a kindly spirit, even with respect to people who transgress the Torah.
>
> 7. An individual ought to refrain from speaking derogatorily about any person; this holds true even with respect to animals.
>
> 10. A person ought to avoid speaking about worldly matters altogether, but should only discuss matters related to Torah.
>
> 11. Let an individual refrain from touching his body with his hand, and from lowering his hand below his navel.
>
> 32. A person ought to meditate upon matters of Torah with each and every bite he eats in order that his food may serve as a sacrifice and his drinking of water and wine as drink-offerings.

In connection with the Safed mystics, we should also note the rules drawn up by Jacob Zemah, disciple of the great kabbalist Isaac Luria, the Ari. These were published as *Shulhan Arukh ha-Ari* (The code of the Ari).[9] Similarly, rules from the Lurianic writings were composed by the Belzer hasid Uri Strelisker and published under the title *Petorta de-Abba* (Jerusalem 1905). Another edition of the latter work was published (Jerusalem 1975) with the title *Minhagey ha-Ari.* At the end of this edition are recorded the rules of the Jerusalem kabbalist Shalom Sharabi (1720–1772).[10] However, the Lurianic and Sharabi rules are not *hanhagot* in the general sense but rather are directions for prayer in the Lurianic–kabbalistic mode. The same applies to Jacob Zemah's other work *Nagid u-Metzavveh.*[11]

RULES FROM THE BESHTIAN HASIDIM

Influenced by these earlier examples, Beshtian Hasidism produced its own *hanhagot.* Recently, a hasidic author, J. D. Weintraub, published a selection of thirty-five of these (*Tzavvaot ve-Hanhagot*) attributed, generally correctly, to particular masters. They could quite easily be multiplied. Virtually every rebbe drew up such rules, and their followers drew up lists of practices that they had themselves observed or of which they had heard.[12]

In typical hasidic vein, and undoubtedly having in mind that the rules are not applicable in their entirety to the ordinary *hasid,*[13] Weintraub writes in his preface:

> These holy rules have been garnered from the writings of the hasidic fathers. They wrote these for their own generation–and for future generations–in order to fan the spark in dry bones, to kindle the flaming fire of the Lord in the souls of Israel. It is our hope that this will be of great advantage to everyone in whose midst is the fear of the Lord. They will bestir themselves from time's slumbers and each will discover some *hanhagah* whereby his heart will be set on fire for the worship of the Lord, blessed be He.

The best known of the hasidic *hanhagot* is the *Tzavvat ha-Ribash* (The Last Will and Testament of the Baal Shem Tov). This classical hasidic work, based on a manuscript belonging to Isaiah Yanover and with additions from the school of the Maggid of Mesirech, was first published in Zolkiew in the late eighteenth century. It has since been issued in numerous editions. Rabbi Shneur Zalman of Liady has noted that the title is a misnomer.[14] The Baal Shem Tov left no ethical will. In any event, scholars have noted, the work is from the school of the Maggid, and it is one of the most influential in Hasidism. A few of the numbered items are cited here.

> 6. It is also essential for man to serve God, blessed be He, with all his strength, but it should all be for the sake of The Most High. For God wishes to be served in all ways. The meaning is that often a man is obliged to converse with others and is unable to study the Torah at that time. Yet he should be attached (*davuk*) to God in his thoughts and

perform unifications (*yihudim*). And so, too, when a man is on a journey and unable to pray and study in his usual way, he is required to serve God in other ways. He should not be distressed by this since God wishes to be served in many different ways; at one time in this, at another time in another. This is the reason why he was moved to travel or to converse with others. It is in order to serve God in that way.

8. He should attach his thoughts on high and he should not eat or drink overmuch and should not give himself pleasure. He should not reflect at all upon worldly matters and should in all things try to keep himself apart from their material aspect. For reflection on the things of this world makes a man coarse. . . .

11. He should never be at all in a state of melancholy because he lacks the ability to satisfy his worldly desires. On the contrary, he should rejoice exceedingly in that he then has the privilege of subduing his lusts for God's sake. . . .

15. Before anything else he should take care that every movement of his body in God's service should be without any ulterior motive, God forbid. Great skill is required in this matter. It is deep, deep; who can find it? Consequently, there is no option but that this should be a permanent reminder, from which the mind never departs for a moment. This is a matter that becomes unfit as soon as the mind is not on it.

26. This is a great principle. Whatever thought he has when he first rises from his bed he should follow that and no other all day.

36. It is by a special act of divine grace that a man remains alive after he has prayed. For in the natural course of events he should have died as a result of the prayers and intentions into which he has put all his vital force.

48. At times the evil inclination leads a man astray by persuading him that he has committed a great sin whereas, in reality, it was only a mere peccadillo or no sin at all. The intention of the evil inclination in all this is to encourage a man to be in a state of melancholy and in that state cease to serve God. A man has to be aware of this cunning trap and he should say to the evil inclination, "That minor offense with which you taunt me does not bother me and you speak falsely. Even if it is truly some slight sin, my Maker will obtain greater satisfaction in that I take no notice of that need for strictness to which you refer, causing me to be sad for God's service. On the contrary, I shall serve Him with joy. For

this is the great principle, that my intention when I worship is not for myself but only to give satisfaction to God. Consequently, though I take no notice of the strictness to which you refer, God will not be offended. For the reason I take no notice is so that I do not cease from serving Him, and how can I cease from serving Him even for a moment?

Appended to the *Noam Elimelekh* of Elimelech of Lizensk are two sets of *hanhagot.* We noted the first of these, the *Tzetil Katan,* earlier.[15] The second is titled *Hanhagot Adam.*

G. Nigal has noted that both these sets of rules are not found in early editions of the *Noam Elimelekh* and, rightly, views with suspicion the attribution of the *Hanhagot Adam* to Elimelech.[16] The *Tzetil Katan* may well be authentic; however, Nigal suggests, it was originally intended not to be part of the *Noam Elimelekh,* but to be read and studied on its own. In any event, the *Hanhagot Adam* is a typical early hasidic-type list of rules, from which a few passages can be quoted here. The list is headed with the formula of the Safed kabbalists,[17] to which it is obviously indebted: "These are the things which if a man practices, he shall live by them."

2. A man must take care to avoid the following: flattery, telling lies, scoffing, malicious gossip, envy, hatred, competition, anger and pride, gazing at women, and conversing idly with a woman even if she is his own wife, especially when she has her periods.

4. Each day he should study in awe and dread some work of reproof: *Reshit Hokhmah, Shelah,* or *Hovot ha-Levavot.*

17. If anyone insults him he should be very glad that God has brought it about so that he might suffer denigration because of his ugly deeds. And every other person should seem to him to be his better.

The following list of *hanhagot* is attributed to R. Yehiel Michel of Zlotchow (1721–1786), disciple of the Baal Shem Tov. Two versions are given in the work *Mayyim Rabbim,* edited by M.N. Kohen of Kolbiel (Warsaw 1891). This list is from the second version.[18]

1. To recite the *Shema* before retiring to sleep as in the work *Shaarey Tzion,* and there should be no interruption between the recitation and going to sleep.

2. To recite the midnight vigil (*Tikkun Hatzot*) every day, whether it be summer or winter, and the appropriate version on the Sabbaths and festivals, even though to do this will leave no time for study afterwards.

3. To recite afterwards many psalms. If it is possible to recite the whole Book of Psalms each week, how goodly and how pleasant.

4. To take care not to speak from the time of rising in the morning until an hour after the prayers, not even to his wife and children, and the same applies to the afternoon and night prayers.

5. Not to gaze outside his four cubits, at least when he goes to the synagogue and when he leaves the synagogue, and it goes without saying while he is actually in the synagogue, unless it is really urgent.

6. Not to walk four cubits without washing his hands in the morning.

7. Also no four cubits without *tzitzit*.

8. To join day to night in study of the Torah.

9. To take care to respond "Amen" after every benediction he hears; otherwise he is under the ban from on high.

10. Not to utter the name of Heaven for no reason. If it happened that he did, a court composed of three should nullify the ban.

11. To take care not to gaze at women or girls or at his own wife when she has her period or at the colored garments of a woman, even when the garments hang on the wall.

12. Not to gossip overmuch with a woman; the Sages said this even with regard to his own wife, especially when she has her period.

13. Not to gaze at any creatures when they are engaged in copulation.

14. To take care to give charity daily and never less than a *perutah*.

15. To take care to study *Mishnah* and *Gemara* daily.

16. To take care to make a promise to give charity before performing the marital act and to give it to the poor on that very day.

17. To take care not to offer his prayers while wearing clothes he has worn during the marital act and to have immersion always after the act, and to fast whenever, God forbid, he has an involuntary emission.

18. To take care to wash the hands before the marital act and after it before going to sleep.

19. To take care not to steal anything worth even a *perutah,* not even from a non-Jew. If he does not know from whom he has stolen something, he should donate the amount for communal purposes.

20. To take care never to put anyone to shame, not even if the man is a notorious sinner.

21. To take care to sleep with a garment containing the fringes, and to take care to study each night before going to sleep a passage from the rabbinic *Aggada* or the *Zohar.*

22. He should not walk between two women and should not allow a woman to walk between him and another man, and he should not walk between two unclean animals.

23. He should be on his guard against malicious gossip, slander, idle talk, scoffing; and from anger and melancholy he should keep afar to the utmost degree.

24. He should pray from a prayerbook with his face to the wall and with concentration and to respond "Amen, may His great Name be magnified" with all his strength and with full concentration and not to speak in the synagogue, especially when the congregation is praying.

25. To take care not to profane the Sabbath even by word.

26. To take care not to eat at night food that increases semen, as mentioned in the *Shelah.*

The majority of these rules are found in other hasidic works.[19] The direct source in one or two is obviously Elimelech of Lizensk. The first version of *Mayyim Rabbim*[20] has a number of variants, but the two versions are basically very similar, with differences only in the wording. In this version, however, number 26 reads "To read this letter (*iggeret*) daily."

RULES FROM THE MAGGID OF MESIRECH

The *hanhagot* attributed to the great organizer and founder of the hasidic movement, Dov Baer, the Maggid of Mesirech, are found in the manuscript version (and at the end of the published work) of *Hayyim va-Hesed,* by R. Hayyim Haikel of Amdur (d. 1787), disciple of the Maggid.[21] In the manuscript they are referred to not as *hanhagot,* but as *kelalim noraim* (tremendous principles). They are essentially a brief statement of the principles of Hasidism as taught in the school of the Maggid. Some excerpts follow:

> A further great principle is for a man to be joyful all the time, since melancholia is a great hindrance to the worship of the Creator. Even if, God forbid, he has committed a sin, he should not be too distressed and so cease from his devotion. All he should do is to be distressed and then get over it to rejoice in the Creator, blessed be He. This is [basically the same as the principle in the *Tzavvat ha-Ribash,* quoted earlier].
>
> Another great principle is that whatever he does he should intend it for the purpose of giving satisfaction to the *Shekhinah,* and he should not have the slightest intention to do it for his own benefit. Even if he does many things and makes many preparations in order to worship with attachment (*devekut*) but his aim is to obtain delight from the act of worship, this, too, is worship for his own ends. But the main thing in all his worship should be for the sake of the *Shekhinah,* and not even a small part should be for himself.
>
> When he rises at midnight and finds himself falling asleep, he should walk about singing, raising his voice in song in order to drive away the sleepiness.
>
> He should have many courses of study. It should not all be in the same subject so that it seems a burden but should be varied.

RULES FROM THE LITHUANIAN-MITNAGGEDIC SCHOOL

The very different Lithuanian-mitnaggedic school produced its own lists of saintly rules. Asher ha-Kohen, disciple of R. Hayyim of Volozhyn, compiled a list of the practices, customs, and maxims he had observed or had heard from R. Hayyim, all based on the way pursued by R. Hayyim's master, the Gaon of Vilna. Some of these rules are ritualistic, having to do with the correct manner of wearing *tefillin, tzitzit,* and so forth. It is interesting that R. Hayyim is said to have remarked that his master, the Gaon, did not wear the *tefillin* of Rabbenu Tam because the law follows Rashi, and the Gaon did not want to waste a minute of his time without *tefillin,* as he would have had to if he had been obliged to take off the Rashi *tefillin* in order to wear those of Rabbenu Tam.[22] *Tefillin* should be worn all day, not only during prayers [no. 15].

R. Hayyim stated that from the day he became responsible for his actions, he always recited his prayers in the synagogue with a quorum present [no. 20]. In what is evidently a gentle dig at the hasidim, R. Hayyim remarked that although the old maxim has it that prayer without concentration is like a body without a soul, yet such prayer, although not equivalent to an animal sacrifice (since the animal has a "soul," or life), it is still accounted as a meal-offering [no. 23]. Prayer must be petitionary, and not only for thanksgiving [no. 24]. It is better to pray calmly and in a spirit of supplication than noisily and with flaming enthusiasm (*hitlahavut* is the favorite hasidic term). The main intention in prayer, even when praying for one's own material and physical needs, should be for the sake of God, who is grieved when there is human suffering [no. 28].

The emphasis in study should be on the Talmud and the Codes. People say that to study the Codes without the Talmud is like eating fish without pepper, but rather, it is like eating pepper without fish [no. 49]. It is no longer permitted to commit a holy sin (i.e., a sin for a good purpose); this was permitted only in former times [no. 132]. Whenever possible, one should keep away from the company of others [no. 144]. Although the Vilna Gaon had an ascent of soul each night without any kabbalistic preparations (*yihudim*), he used to say that this was not an ideal, since it was in the nature of a reward (Tales, no. 2). In Tales, no. 5, the Gaon is referred to as *he-hasid.* A young girl performed miracles and spoke of marvelous things. She studied the Zohar and great secret teachings with the scholars. The Gaon said that when she married, the spirit would depart from her, and so it was (Tales, no. 8). R. Hayyim said that whatever the Baal Shem Tov knew, he attained through requests in dreams (Tales, no. 13).

It is easy to see in all this the conscious reaction of the Vilna Gaon's school to the saintly life as understood by Hasidism. The supernatural aspects of saintliness are emphasized in the school of the Gaon, as they are in Hasidism, but the former appears to be a more sober approach, if any saintly path can be described as sober.

RULES FROM THE MUSAR MOVEMENT

Glenn[23] has shown how R. Israel Salanter, the founder of the Musar movement, used the work *Heshbon ha-Nefesh,* by Mendel Lefin (1742–1819), which is based on Benjamin Franklin's autobiography! Franklin's "thirteen virtues and thirteen precepts" were used by the Musarists as aids in their quest for self-improvement. These are:

1. temperance
2. silence
3. order
4. resolution
5. frugality
6. industry
7. sincerity
8. justice
9. moderation
10. cleanliness
11. tranquility
12. chastity
13. humility

These qualities, in themselves, can hardly be called ways of saintliness for they are ethical rather than religious precepts, and they arise from a Western, Christian background. For instance, on "humility," Franklin says, "Imitate Jesus and Socrates." The point is, however, that the Musarists used these and similar prescriptions in pursuit of Jewish religious values, as a means toward the worship of God with an inward focus. In this respect the principles can certainly be embraced by the term saintly *hanhagot;* they are different from the kabbalistic and hasidic *hanhagot* only in method and content, not in aim. The purpose is the same – the proper worship of God.

Dov Katz, in his *Tenuat ha-Musar,* provides lists of *hanhagot* that the Musarists drew up for themselves. These, unlike the kabbalistic, hasidic, and Salanter types, are intimate and personal, aimed at the improvement of the individual character.

A particularly revealing example is provided in the diary of R. Nathan Zvi Finkel (1849–1927), founder of the Slabodka (Lithuania) school of Musar.[24] R. Ezekiel Sarna discovered a notebook in the loft of a house in Slabodka, and he recognized from the handwriting that it had been composed by R. Finkel. Evidently out of fear that it might be seen by others, Finkel had written his diary in code. Katz has published this remarkable document. Following are a few passages as decoded by Katz with the help of Finkel's disciples:

> You must take excessive care to keep and to rehearse all that you have taken upon yourself until now. The main thing is for you to take counsel with a man great in Torah and the fear of Heaven regarding M [either Musar or *middot,* "character traits"] and in the matter of self-scrutiny. Remember all this. Forget it not.

> You must take care with regard to (1) that which the Sages say (*Bava Batra* 8a), "Charity must be distributed by three persons." (2) To make an assessment of your actions to the utmost degree. (3) To be as careful as you possibly can not to put another to shame. (4) The study of Musar should be such that produces practical results and makes constant demands on yourself.

> Have you kept to your sacred resolve to study Musar daily from a book? Have you reflected on man and his obligations at least once a month? With really profound reflection?

> Especially you must make demands on yourself to realize all the above. Remember, forget it not, to reveal your secrets to yourself in breadth and with boldness in order that you do not stumble so as to fool others and a fortiori never to try to fool God. Take constant assessment to see whether you have not stumbled in this matter, Heaven forfend, in word or thought and without taking counsel of the great teacher [mentioned above].

> Have you been suspicious of yourself? Have you not overlooked the fact that you are unworthy of the post you occupy (as the head of the

yeshivah)? And so with regard to many other matters. Have you been careful to the utmost degree? Answer with your mouth, not only in your heart.

Have you kept the vow you made when in trouble, Heaven save us, to fast three days in winter? You must remember it, for it is a very serious matter.

RULES OF THE COLLEGE IN KELME

R. Simhah Zissel Broida (1824–1898), chief disciple of R. Israel Salanter, founded a theological college in Kelme, in Lithuania, in which young men studied to become both expert talmudists and practitioners of the Musar discipline.[25] The students at this school drew up and agreed to follow a number of rules. Although they are hardly rules for saints, they are relevant to our subject. The rules require one to:

Strive for prayer to be in the Musar spirit.

Take hold of some spiritual maxim and rehearse it regularly.

Set aside at least twice a week a period in which to become accustomed to the effect of reflection on the character.

Reflect at least twice a week on the spending of words, which should be as hard as spending one's money.

Accustom oneself, at least once a week, to rise from one's bed energetically to worship God, like soldiers who rise energetically to serve their country.

These and similar *hanhagot* of the Lithuanian school are more sober, more intellectual, and less extravagant in piety than those found in the Safed and hasidic lists. Nevertheless, it is probable that the very idea of compiling lists of *hanhagot* was introduced in this school under the influence of the earlier examples of the genre.

There are a number of accounts from the Hungarian school regarding the special devotional and pietistic customs of the *Hatam Sofer.*[26] The following are more in the nature of impressions gathered from the saint's family and disciples than direct testimony; they obviously must be taken with a grain of salt, but they are revealing nonetheless of the type of *hasidut* pursued by those of the Hungarian school.[27]

> From the day he was responsible for his actions, he never had extraneous thoughts during his prayers.
>
> He used to pray with burning enthusiasm (*hitlahavut*) and take a long time over his prayers.
>
> All his days he never had any ulterior motive when he taught the Torah in public (that is, thoughts of pride or desire to win fame).
>
> In all his numerous Responsa he never tried to parade his learning, only to clarify the truth for its own sake.
>
> From the age of 10 he never walked four cubits without Torah and the fear of God, and no day passed without his discovering new ideas in the Torah.
>
> He hid from people his great knowledge of the Kabbalah.
>
> Apart from his valet, nobody ever saw him without his overcoat.
>
> He ate only light food, and when he realized that food put before him was tasty, he put it away.
>
> His coffee and soup were always so hot that nobody else would have been able to drink them. His bathwater, too, was always boiling hot.
>
> He was always the first to greet others.

We have considered many types of saintly conduct in this chapter. Varied though they are, they all exhibit the kind of extreme piety that can be termed, without distortion, saintliness.

8

SAINTLY POWERS

Jewish pietists have always believed that holy men possessed supernatural powers. The biblical model was the prophet, especially Elijah and Elisha, and the Bible tells of miracles wrought on their behalf. The Talmud contains tales of the saints emulating the biblical miracle workers. R. Phinehas b. Yair, for example, causes a river to be parted so that he can pass through it on his way to ransom captives. His power, it is said, was greater than that of Moses and his people. For them, the sea was only parted once, but for R. Phinehas it was parted three times – for the saint himself and for two companions, one of whom was a Gentile (*Hullin* 10b). The Emperor Antoninus is said to have acknowledged the miraculous powers of a disciple of R. Judah the Prince, who brought one of the emperor's slain guards back to life (*Avodah Zarah* 10b). R. Hanina b. Dosa used to pray for the sick to be healed and was able to foretell whether his prayer for a particular person would be answered (Mishnah *Berakhot* 5:5). The third chapter of tractate *Taanit* in the Babylonian Talmud contains a number of tales in which Honi the Circle Drawer, Abba Hilkiah, his grandson, and other saints perform startling miracles, especially when praying for rain. The medieval authors called this chapter *pirka de-hasidey,* "the chapter of the saints."[1]

BELIEF IN MIRACLES

The legendary nature of these rabbinic tales is obvious, and in some instances, the rabbis who told them might themselves have treated them as no more than pious legend.[2] But that is not the whole story. The belief persisted that holy men were capable of overriding the claims of the natural order by the powers God had given them as a reward for their holy ways. The element of Oriental hyperbole should not be discounted, but behind all the stories is the firm belief in the miraculous powers of the saint. The philosophical discussion of whether miracles are possible, includes Hume's observation that it is basically a question of whether the evidence for the alleged miracle is reliable. The matter has been investigated, in more recent times, from the point of view of parapsychology.[3] However, these deliberations are tangential to our inquiry, which is concerned not with whether the saints actually possessed supernatural powers, but with whether they were *believed* to possess them. The general attitude is well expressed in a hasidic saying about the miracles alleged to have been performed by the zaddikim: Anyone who believes that these things actually happened is stupid; but anyone who believes that they could not possibly have happened is an *epikoros* (heretic).

A kindred question is whether the rabbis acknowledged that there is an element of vulgarity in the appeal to miracles. In this connection, both Sevin[4] and Urbach[5] quote the talmudic account (*Shabbat* 53b) of the poor man whose wife had died, leaving him with an infant who had to be fed. Miraculously, the man's breasts became like those of a woman, and he was able to nurse the infant. Hearing this, R. Joseph remarked, "How great this man must have been that such a miracle should have been performed on his behalf."

But Abbaye retorted, "On the contrary! How unworthy this man must have been that the order of creation was changed on his behalf."

Surely Abbaye was not challenging the principle that the holy man can perform miracles; otherwise, why did he issue his challenge only in this instance? Abbaye's suggestion of unworthiness would seem to apply only to this situation, either because the man had no reputation for holy living (Urbach's conclusion) or, more likely because, unlike the answers to prayers for the rains to come, this miracle was "unnatural" in that it resulted in a reversal of male and female roles. God has created rain, so even when it comes as a result of the saint's prayers, no overturning of the laws of nature (*sidrey bereshit* in the teminology of the Talmud) is involved; in contrast, because God created males to be different from females, it is contrary to the divine plan for a man to have female breasts. The implication is that not all supernatural events are brought about by the powers of the holy man who does the will of God.

It is interesting in this connection that during the Middle Ages, the popular view among Jews was that Jesus really did perform his miracles, but that he did so by means of magic.[6] Similarly, many did not deny that the false Messiah, Shabbatai Zevi, performed miracles, but, it was suggested, he used the black arts to perform them.[7] In a prescientific age, the whole idea that nature's laws were fixed was unknown. Indeed, there was no concept of natural law at all. What seems to be the natural order, it was held, could be overturned on occasion, either by the holy powers of the saint or the unholy powers of the magician.

Even the philosophical rationalists in the Middle Ages did not deny the powers possessed by the person whose life is centered on God. Maimonides (*Guide,* III, 51) said that such a person could safely pass through fire and water, although Maimonides limits this capacity to be immune from all mishaps to the very few. Moreover, Maimonides is silent on the question of whether the holy man's divine protective powers can extend beyond himself to others.

BANEFUL POWERS

The powers of the saint were occasionally exercised in a baneful manner. The Mishnah (*Avot* 2:10) records Rabbi Eliezer as saying, "Warm thyself by the fire of the wise; but beware of their glowing coals, lest thou be burnt, for their bite is the bite of the fox, and their sting is the scorpion's sting, and their hiss is the serpent's hiss, and all their words are like coals of fire." Singer's rationalistic interpretation of this passage is banal:[8] "The holiest gifts, if abused, may prove a source of suffering to those they are designed to benefit." In context, the meaning is, as in similar talmudic passages, that treating holy men (here *hakhamim*, "sages") in too familiar a fashion can invoke their displeasure and bring harm to the offender. The passage refers to the numinous power of the sacred, and the danger of drawing near to it, as when Uzziah was stricken (2 Samuel 6:7) when he touched the Ark of God.[9]

In another talmudic story (*Bava Metzia* 84a), R. Johanan was distressed by what he considered to be an insolent remark made to him by his colleague, Resh Lakish. Shortly thereafter, Resh Lakish became ill and died as a result of R. Johanan's displeasure. Of the same R. Johanan, on the other hand, it is told that by giving his hand to another sick colleague, R. Eleazar, he enabled the sick man to rise from his bed, completely cured (*Berakhot* 5b).

There are a number of instances in which the holy man's baneful gaze at a sinner reduces the sinner to "a heap of bones" (*Berakhot* 58a, *Shabbat* 34a, *Bava Batra* 75a). Later Jewish hagiography contains numerous tales about holy men destroying by their numinous power tyrants who oppressed the Jews. But there are also tales of Jews themselves coming to harm and even death because something they had said or done had displeased or offended a saint. To this day some continue to fear annoying or speaking ill of holy men (even when they are no longer alive).

Israel Klepholtz remarks that some of the hasidim of the Belzer rebbe, R. Arele (1880–1957), attributed the death of R. Mechele, one of the rebbe's *gabbaim* (administrators of the rebbe's "court"), to the fact that he once complained to the rebbe about the *yoshevim* ("sitters," *hasidim* who spent a monastic life in Belz).[10] The angry rebbe cried out, "I can manage quite well with only a single gabbai." R. Mechele, witnessing the rebbe's displeasure, took off his shoes and, with bitter tears, begged the rebbe to forgive him. "I wish I could," the rebbe said, "but I cannot take back my words." The gabbai went home, became ill, and died within a few days. Klepholtz concludes his weird tale: "His aged father and the hasidim wept for him, declaring, 'R. Mechele has been burned by the coals of our master.' "

Implied in this and many similar stories is that the saint himself must be careful to control his powers, just as a physically strong man must know his own strength. If a gentle saint like R. Arele, who, it was said, would never willingly hurt a fly, were to let slip a few words of displeasure, he would be unable to withdraw them, despite the knowledge that they would bring about disastrous unintended results. A. Levi sees it necessary to remark at the beginning of his biography of R. Yosef Dayyan:[11]

> I know my own unworthiness and my intellectual poverty so that I am unable to penetrate to the profundities of the subject, the wondrous deeds of the saints (*tzaddikim*) quoted in this book. If I have erred and have not been sufficiently careful in the language I have used adequately to delineate their words and wondrous deeds, I beg the saints to forgive me and not allow their displeasure to affect me, my family or anyone in Israel.

Even among the non-hasidic Jews of Russia and Lithuania, home of the *mitnaggedim,* who were always ready to scoff at the extreme veneration of the *hasidim* for their rebbes, the fear of the saint's displeasure and the harm that could result from it was extended to the local traditional rabbi of the community. Tchernowitz relates in his autobiography that his grandfather, a prominent Russian rabbi, discovered that some members of his community had stolen from the non-Jews in the town.[12] When they came to trial in the Russian court, they took false oaths, thereby profaning the Divine Name. The rabbi cursed them to the effect that they should not live out the year, and some of them did indeed die within that year. One of them declared on his deathbed, "*Nu!* If the rabbi has ordered us to die, then die we must." Tchernowitz adds, "Naturally, the older generation considered it to be a miracle, but that is how it happened."[13]

THE SAINT AS MIRACLE WORKER

The role of the saint as miracle worker was stressed particularly in Beshtian Hasidism.[14] The hasidic *zaddik* both guides his followers in the spiritual path and performs miracles, especially of healing, on their behalf. The founder of the movement, the Baal Shem Tov, "Master of the Good Name," was so called because of his use of various divine names for healing purposes. In his day there were many *baaley shem* who had convinced the masses that they could effect cures through their knowledge of the practical Kabbalah (i.e., the use of the names of God and the angels found in the kabbalistic works for magical purposes, albeit for white magic). It is true that the Baal Shem Tov was primarily a charismatic leader who assisted his followers in their quest for holy living. In later hasidic lore it is this aspect of the Baal Shem Tov's personality that is stressed, and his role as a *baal shem* is played down considerably, as if the hasidim were embarrassed by it. It is also true that in some versions of Hasidism–Kotz and Habad, for example–the miraculous aspects of zaddikism are relegated to the background. For all that, no version of Hasidism rejects entirely the role of the *zaddik* as miracle worker. In some versions of the movement this is his chief role. There are a number of rebbes who are given the title *baal mofet*, "master of miracles." In the battle between the hasidim and the *maskilim*, the followers of the Enlightenment movement, the latter were critical of the obscurantism, as they saw it, of the *zaddikim* and their followers. Instead of consulting skilled physicians when they were ill, the *maskilim* claimed, the hasidim tended to rely on the healing powers of the rebbe. This is one of the reasons for the dubbing of physicians as heretics in a good deal of hasidic or hasidic-inspired literature.

Especially through his prayers on their behalf, the *zaddik* was able to help his followers.[15] Passages in the talmudic literature are drawn on heavily by the Hasidim in justification. Once the term *zaddik* had come to be used to denote the saint instead of, as originally, simply the good man,[16] passages in which the word *tzaddik* occurs were used to convey ideas about the spiritual powers of the *zaddik* in the new sense. Thus the talmudic saying (*Moed Katan* 16b) that while God decrees, the *zaddik* can nullify the decree, was intended to imply that God has delivered into the hands of the *zaddik* the power to control the divine Providence.[17] Another talmudic passage that shifts through reinterpretation is the saying of Rava (*Moed Katan* 28a), "Life, children, and sustenance depend not on merit but on *mazzal*." In this context, *mazzal* denotes *fate, destiny*, or *fortune*. In the hasidic interpretation, however, the word is connected with the root *to flow*. The flow of the divine grace is promoted by the prayers of the *zaddik* on behalf of his followers rather than by their own merits.[18] Hasidic thought similarly reinterprets the talmudic saying (*Berakhot* 17b) that in the days of R.

Hanina b. Dosa, a heavenly voice proclaimed, "The whole world is sustained because of (*bishvil*) Hanina, my son." The word is taken to mean "in the *shevil*"; that is, in the channel, or conduit. The *zaddik* is the channel through which the divine grace flows to nourish the world.[19] There are innumerable hasidic tales in which the rebbe effects miraculous cures after the doctors had thrown up their hands in despair, or in which the rebbe succeeds, by the power of his prayers, in enabling a childless couple to be blessed with children. Another motif in the hasidic tales is that of the dead saint whose corpse is taken to the *mikveh* for the final purification and the saint dips himself, dead though he is.[20]

There are also tales of the *zaddikim* possessing prophetic powers.[21] R. Jacob Isaac of Lublin (1745–c. 1815) was known as the seer because of his clairvoyant powers. The seer is said to have noted to young Hayyim Halberstam (later the Zaddik of Zans) that the *zaddik* is like the high priest who consults the *Urim ve-Tumim.* Now that we no longer have the *Urim ve-Tumim,* it is possible for the *zaddik* to see the letters of the Tetragrammaton shining in the Torah, and this enables him to give proper counsel to his followers.[22] There are hasidic tales about the attempt by the seer and his colleagues to aid Napoleon in his battle with Russia by means of mystical exercises (*yihudim*). Martin Buber's novel *For the Sake of Heaven* is based on this episode.

From the beginnings of Hasidism enormous claims were made for the *zaddikim,* as we have seen. The *zaddikim* were said to have been gifted with the holy spirit, possessed of unparalleled spiritual power and able to perform the most extraordinary miracles. Such claims, as the opponents of the movement were quick to point out, were in flat contradiction to what had become virtually a dogma long before the age that saw the rise of Hasidism, that the generations exhibit a progressive decline as they are distanced in time from the revelation at Sinai. According to this doctrine, later teachers are bound to be spiritually inferior to the ancients. We must here examine the doctrine and see how Hasidism coped with the apparent contradiction.

One of the talmudic texts in this connection refers specifically to miracle working (*Berakhot* 20a):

> R. Pappa asked Abbaye, "Why is it that miracles were performed for those of former generations but no miracles are performed for us? It

> cannot be because they were superior in their studies, since in the days of R. Judah all their efforts were concentrated on the tractate *Nezikin,* whereas we study all the Six Orders. And when R. Judah came to tractate *Uktzin* in the law 'If a woman presses vegetables' (according to others, to the law 'Olives pressed with their leaves are clean'), he would declare, 'I see here the kind of problem raised by Rav and Samuel,' whereas we have thirteen different versions of *Uktzin.* And yet when R. Judah drew off a single shoe the rains would come, whereas we torment ourselves and cry out loudly and not the slightest notice is taken of us."
>
> Abbaye replied, "The former generations were ready to sacrifice themselves for the sanctification of the divine name, whereas we are not ready to sacrifice ourselves for the sanctification of the divine name."

The passage concludes with a story illustrating an earlier saint's readiness for self-sacrifice.

In this passage, the power to work miracles through prayer depends on readiness for self-sacrifice for the sake of God; it is implied that the talmudic giants, Abbaye and R. Pappa, were incapable of this degree of selflessness and hence could not perform miracles. Since Abbaye and R. Pappa said this about themselves and their contemporaries, it would seem to follow a priori that it applied to the post-talmudic teachers, and yet the hasidim claimed that the masters could change the course of nature by the power of their prayers.

THE ANCIENTS VERSUS THE CONTEMPORARIES

It is worth noting that in the foregoing text, while the earlier teachers are said to be superior in sanctity and in the resulting power to work miracles, it is the later teachers who are actually superior in learning. The idea that a necessary and progressive decline of the generations does not apply to learning is also implied in the oft-quoted statement in the Mishnah (*Eduyot* 1:5) that a court can set aside the ruling of an earlier court only if the later court is superior "in wisdom and numbers," suggesting that it is possible for the later court to be superior in learning. It was not until the Middle Ages, by which time the idea of progressive decline had acquired the force of dogma, that it came to be held without question that a later court could never be superior to an earlier one in wisdom, at least so far as the "court" of the talmudic rabbis was concerned.

That the later generations are necessarily inferior to the ancients is stated in another talmudic passage (*Yoma* 9b).

> R. Johanan said, "The fingernails of the former generations [i.e., those who lived before the destruction of the Temple] are better than the stomachs of the later ones."
>
> Said Resh Lakish to him, "On the contrary, the later ones are superior, since despite their subordination to the [Roman] government, they still study the Torah."
>
> R. Johanan replied, "Let the Temple be the proof. It was restored to the earlier ones but it has not been restored to the later ones."
>
> They asked R. Eleazar, "Which are greater, the earlier or the later ones?"
>
> He replied, "Set your eyes on the Temple." (Others say, "The Temple is your proof.")

In another passage (*Eruvin* 53a) the learning of the *Amoraim* is adversely compared to that of the *Tannaim*.

> R. Johanan said, "The heart of the earlier ones was open like the entrance to the outer hall of the Temple, while the heart of the later teachers was only open like the entrance to the inner hall [which was smaller]. But as for us, the opening is no bigger than the eye of a fine needle." By the earlier ones, Rabbi Akiba is meant; by the later ones, Rabbi Eleazar b. Shamua is meant. (Others say that by the earlier ones, Rabbi Eleazar b. Shamua is meant, and by the later ones, Rabbi Oshia Beribi.)
>
> Abbaye said, "We are like a peg in the wall with regard to Gemara."
>
> Rava said, "We are like a finger in wax with regard to Sevara."
>
> R. Ashi said, "We are like a finger in a pit with regard to forgetfulness."

The most influential passage, however, is one known to every student of the Talmud. It is the one usually quoted for the doctrine of the decline of the generations (*Shabbat* 112b): R. Zera said that Rava bar Zamina said,

> If the early ones were like angels, then we are like human beings. But if the early ones were like human beings, then we are like donkeys; not like the donkey of R. Hanina b. Dosa or the donkey of R. Phinehas b. Yair, but like ordinary donkeys.

By the Middle Ages, these passages, especially the latter, had acquired the full force and authority of the Talmud, the final court of appeal for rabbinic Judaism not only in matters of law but in all religious matters. The Zohar (III, 2a), obviously relying on passages such as these, extends the doctrine to mystical thought, the later mystics being considered inferior to the earlier adepts in both mystical knowledge and experience of the divine.

The medieval Jewish teachers, refusing to allow themselves to become completely stultified by the dogma of decline, adopted various ploys to defend their right to originality. The best known of these is the famous illustration of the pygmy standing on the shoulders of a giant. Indeed, later teachers were pygmies in relation to the giants of the past, but because they had the shoulders of the ancients upon which to stand, they could perceive vistas quite impossible for them if they had stood on their own two feet.[23]

A suggestion that the later mystics possessed greater insights than the ancients is advanced in the work *Berit Menuhah,* attributed to Abraham of Granada.[24] It is only those who come midway between the ancients and the very latest mystics who are necessarily inferior. This is because there are cycles of mystic power, just as there are cycles in nature. Just as the planets eventually come full circle in the revolution of the great sphere, so it is with regard to mystical wisdom. The revolution is complete by the age of the latest teachers, so that it is possible for a very late teacher to be endowed with greater spiritual and mystical awareness even than the earlier teachers.

For Maimonides, the talmudic rabbis had less knowledge of astronomy than did the gentile scholars of their day.[25] The Geonim believed that the talmudic rabbis had only the poor medical knowledge of their day, so that remedies found in the Talmud should not be relied upon unless contemporary physicians concurred.[26] For all that, very few eighteenth-century Eastern European Jews were prepared to compromise in any way on the view that no post-talmudic teacher could be compared to the spiritual heroes and saints of the Talmud. This was the problem Hasidism had to face. One repeatedly finds in the anti-hasidic polemics of the *mitnaggedim* the complaint that greater claims are made for the *zaddikim* than for the saints of old, as if the *zaddikim* were superior, despite the fact that, as contemporaries, they were bound to be inferior.

An early hasidic reply is to be found in the letter by Eleazar, son of R. Elimelech of Lizensk.[27] Eleazar published his father's work, *Noam Elimelekh,* in 1788, a year after Elimelech's death. Eleazar added to the work a letter in defense of Zaddikism. Eleazar observes that even the opponents of Hasidism admit that the saints of old were gifted with the holy spirit and were able to perform miracles; they argue, however, that such things are no longer possible. Eleazar contends that this is simply because saints are rarely acknowledged as such by their contemporaries. Even Isaac Luria, the Ari, was criticized in his day, and yet all now acknowledge his great sanctity. As it says in the Talmud, (*Hullin* 7b), the righteous are greater when dead than when alive. It appears that to be acknowledged as a holy man, one has first to die; such as accolade is given only posthumously.

It is even suggested, in the name of Elimelech, that it is far easier to attain to the holy spirit "nowadays" than in times of yore. This is because the *Shekhinah* is now in exile and consequently very near. Elimelech quotes the parable given by the Maggid of Rovno (i.e., the Maggid of Mesirech, at that time residing in Rovno).[28] When the king is in his palace, he will leave it only to stay for a while in a splendid mansion where he can be given full regal honors. But when the king is traveling, he is prepared to enter the humblest of dwellings provided it is clean and he is offered hospitality.

A novel defense is offered in the name of R. Phinehas of Koretz, disciple of the Baal Shem Tov.[29] Abraham Ibn Ezra, R. Phinehas is reported to have said, is not to be blamed for his rationalism in daring to criticize such ancient teachers as Kalir, believed to be a *Tanna.* The *Tannaim,* who lived not long after the destruction of the Temple, were able to avail themselves of the tremendous spiritual light shining from the Temple, even though it had already begun to wane. The medieval teachers, like Ibn Ezra, did not have the benefit of the Temple's illumination because by that time the light had waned completely. But contemporary *zaddikim,* while even more distant from the Temple's illumination, are very close to the dawning light of the messianic age. Distant in time, and hence "late" in relation to the illuminations of the past, the zaddikim are very near and thus "early" so far as the greater illuminations of the future are concerned. One would have to be blind, R. Phinehas is reported to have added, not to see the dawning light of the Messiah.

A slightly more elaborate defense is found in the editor's introduction to *Imrey Kodesh,*[30] the collected teachings of Uri of Strelisk (d. 1826). The editor, who is not named, remarks that it is over 130 years since Uri's death, so it is obvious that he is writing around 1956; thus it is somewhat dubious to use what he says for our purpose. On the other hand, he seems to be recording authentic traditions current in the Strelisker school. After referring to the talmudic passages about the decline of the generations, the editor quotes the statement of Abraham of Granada, "The later sages *are greater than the earlier ones*" (italics in original). He also quotes R. Phinehas of Koretz, as noted in the previous paragraph, and concludes:

> Since this is so it is no cause for surprise that we see, after the darkness which prevailed in the Middle Ages, when the light was concealed and every vision blocked, all generations becoming progressively inferior, that the Lord should have illumined our way, that a star should have arisen in Jacob, whose illumination has spread throughout the earth, namely, Israel's light and holy one, the Baal Shem Tov, may his merits shield us. He is the man, the great lion of the forest on high. He ascended the heights to become the disciple of Ahijah the Shilonite, who had heard the Torah from Moses our teacher himself, on whom be peace. After all those generations the wheel has come full circle so that they are able to draw the holy spirit from its Source and the word of the Lord has spread everywhere.

The miracle-working aspect of Zaddikism is generally diminished in the Strelisker school, so there is no reference to it here. However, the problem the author seeks to solve is essentially the same:

How can later generations be superior in spiritual illumination to the ancients? The author, as a true *hasid* of Strelisk, goes on to trace the spiritual genealogy of the *zaddikim* from the Maggid of Mesirech through to his disciple, Solomon of Lutzk, and through Solomon to his disciple, Uri of Strelisk.

A full-scale treatment of the problem is found in Israel Berger's introduction to his *Eser Orot,*[31] a collection of tales of various *zaddikim.* Conscious that even among faithful Jews there is opposition to the institution of Zaddikism, Berger feels obliged to consider the following four objections:

1. Where do we find in classical sources of Judaism that saints can change the laws of nature as radically as the *zaddikim* reportedly did?
2. Even if such things were possible for the ancients, how could they be possible today in view of the talmudic statements regarding the inevitable decline of the generations?
3. What basis is there for the strange methods of biblical exegesis pursued by the *zaddikim*?
4. How can the *zaddikim* possess supernatural powers if some of them are unlearned in Talmud and Codes?

Berger's reply to the third and fourth questions, although interesting, are not germane to this chapter. In reply to the first objection, Berger has no difficulty producing a list of miracle tales from the Talmud and other sources to show that the saints can override nature. In reply to the second objection, Berger advances the following arguments:

First, he contends, the *Amoraim* who spoke of the decline of the generations were not making any kind of dogmatic or categorical statement but, in their humility, were thinking only as it applied to them personally. All they were saying was that they themselves were inferior to the ancients, not that all men in their day were inferior. Second, even if the statements *were* applied to the whole of their generation, it would still be plausible to suggest that they allowed exceptions to the rule. They were not declaring that it is impossible for the later ones to have possessed supernatural powers, only that such powers were rare. Third, Berger quotes Abraham of Granada: There is a fresh outburst of spiritual power once the wheel has come full circle. Fourth, Berger advances a novel thesis. It is known, he remarks, from the Lurianic Kabbalah, that in an age of acute spiritual decline God sends down to earth a most elevated soul that may have gone through successive incarnations, acquiring greater illumination each time. Thus, neatly but artificially, Berger tries to have it both ways. True, the ancient saints were greatly superior to the later saints, but the *zaddikim,* having the souls of ancient saints, actually belonged to the former immaculate generations and have been sent back to earth only to illuminate the way for the poor sinners of these later generations.

THE ORIENTAL SAINTS

Oriental Jews did not lag far behind in their belief in the powers of their saints. The cult of saints in Islam had long had an important influence on the Jews in Islamic lands, but the influence of Hasidism should not be overlooked. The fulsome biographies of contemporary Oriental saints – Mordecai Sharabi, Savaani, Abuchatzeirah, and Yosef Sholomo Dayyan – are full of miracle tales, some of which are so fantastic that it is hard to believe that the most fervent hasid would dare tell them of his rebbe.[32] In the approbation to the Dayyan volume, R. Benjamin Zeev Hashin remarks, "As is well known, the Baal Shem Tov said that so great a thing is it to tell the tales about the zaddikim that it is considered the equivalent of being engaged in the Work of the Chariot."[33] The Abuchatzeirah volume tells that the saint left the town of Yabneh, where he had resided happily, to live in Netivot, only because a Lithuanian talmudist had spoken somewhat disparagingly of the Baal Shem Tov's preference for piety over learning.[34] In the same volume, Mordecai Sharabi is reported to have said that the spiritual power of Abuchatzeirah is equal to that possessed by the Baal Shem Tov, and that if anyone wishes to know what the Baal Shem Tov looked like, he had only to gaze at the face of Abuchatzeirah.[35]

Among the miracles said to have been performed regularly by

Abuchatzeirah was the miracle of the arak.[36] The saint would cover the bottle of arak from which he served his guests and would pour out glass after glass, but the bottle suffered no diminution. In the Rafaeli volume on Sharabi, it is said that the grandfather of the saint used to fly through the air every Sabbath eve from his home in the Yemen to Jerusalem in order to visit the Western Wall.[37] Folktales about flying saints among Oriental Jews are obviously influenced by similar folk beliefs in the ability of the Islamic saints to fly to distant places. It was believed that specially inspired persons could see these saints flying on noble steeds.[38] Jewish saints had no steeds, noble or otherwise. The Dayyan volume tells how this saint uttered certain kabbalistic charms over the sword of a friendly Bedouin shepherd whose flock had regularly been savaged by wolves.[39] Needless to say, the sheep were safe from that day on.

Legends abounded of the miraculous powers of the Moroccan saint Hayyim Attar.[40] He is said to have been able to see from one end of the world to the other and to have had regular visits by the prophet Elijah. A curious legend reports that the saint, traveling in a caravan, was threatened by a fierce lion. The saint uncovered his penis and the lion bolted away in terror. The saint explained to his companions that he had never had a sinful seminal emission, so the holy sign of the covenant had cast dread upon the lion.

EXORCISM

The belief in the saint's power to exorcise evil spirits is ancient.[41] In Chapters 10 and 14 of his *Nishmat Hayyim,* Manasseh b. Israel has a number of stories of saints who exorcised *dybbukim* (evil spirits or souls of the dead pursued by evil spirits) when they had invaded bodies of the living. Here, too, these saintly powers were accepted in the Lithuanian-Mitnaggedic circles as well as by the hasidim. On Purim, Rabbi Elhanan Wasserman (1875–1941) used to tell his disciples of the exorcism by the Hafetz Hayyim in the year 1900, at which he, Elhanan, had been present.[42]

In this and similar matters having to do with the power of the saints, the beliefs transcended the usual divisions of kabbalists, hasidim, Orientals, and Lithuanians.

9

HOW THE SAINTS DIED

On the verse "And Moses the servant of the Lord died there in the land of Moab *by the mouth of the Lord*" (Deuteronomy 34:5), the Talmud (*Bava Batra* 17a) comments that Moses died by a kiss. This became the source of the idea that the soul of the saint leaves the body painlessly at the time of death, returning to its source as if it had been kissed by God. Maimonides (*Guide,* III, 51) understands this to mean that the saint becomes so attached to the Divine during his lifetime that he effortlessly leaves his body behind at his death. As Maimonides puts it, "When a perfect man is stricken with years and approaches death, his apprehension increases very powerfully, joy over this apprehension becomes stronger, until the soul is separated from the body in this state of pleasure."[1] Maimonides implies that only a very few experience this state, but in the hagiographical literature of Judaism, *mitat neshikah,* "death by a divine kiss," is often said to have been the fate of all the saints. In any event, the saint's death is described as the greatest moment of his life on earth.

In addition to the numerous legends woven around the death of Moses and the patriarchs, two events in the older literature provided the material for the later hagiographies: the account of the death of

Rabbi Judah the Prince in the Talmud, and the account of the death of Rabbi Simeon b. Yohai in the Zohar.

JUDAH THE PRINCE

The lengthy passage on the death of Rabbi Judah (*Ketubot* 103a–104a) contains incidental references to the deaths of the saints in general. Rabbi Judah, it is here said, was found weeping at his imminent demise. His disciple, R. Hiyya, asked him, "Is it not taught, If a man dies smiling, it is a good omen for him; if weeping, it is a bad omen for him; his face upwards, it is a good omen; his face downwards, it is a bad omen; his face towards the public, it is a good omen; towards the wall, it is a bad omen; if his face is greenish, it is a bad omen; if bright and ruddy, it is a good omen; dying on Sabbath eve, it is a good omen; on the termination of the Sabbath, it is a bad omen; on the eve of Yom Kippur, it is a bad omen; on the termination of Yom Kippur, it is a good omen; dying of diarrhea is a good omen because most *tzaddikim* die of diarrhea?"

Rabbi Judah replied, "I weep on account of my separation from the Torah and the *mitzvot.*"

The scholars and the populace were praying that Rabbi Judah should be spared when his maidservant went onto the roof and said, "The immortals want Rabbi to join them, and the mortals want Rabbi to remain on earth. May it be the will of God that the mortals prevail." But when she saw Rabbi Judah's great distress, she altered her prayer to request that the immortals should prevail. The passage concludes with a saying attributed to R. Eleazar: "When a righteous man departs from the world he is welcomed by three companies of ministering angels. One exclaims, 'Come into peace'; one exclaims, 'He who walketh in righteousness' (Isaiah 57:2); and one exclaims, 'He shall enter into peace, they shall rest on their beds' (Isaiah 57:2)."

SIMEON BAR YOHAI

A well-known poetic passage in the Zohar vividly describes the death of its supposed author, Rabbi Simeon b. Yohai (Zohar, *Idra Zuta,* III,

287–296). After expounding to his chosen disciples on the most profound heavenly mysteries, Rabbi Simeon expires in glory with fire all around. A voice is heard proclaiming, "Come, gather ye together for the wedding (*hilula*) of Rabbi Simeon." On the basis of this passage, the death of the saint came to be referred to as his *hilula.* The actual meaning of this Aramaic word is *celebration,* particularly of a wedding. In the Talmud (*Ketubot* 62b) the expression "*hilula* of Rabbi Simeon b. Yohai" refers, in fact, to Rabbi Simeon's wedding. It is in the Zohar that the term is first applied to the saint's departure from this earth and the wedding of his soul to the celestial realms.

Benjamin Mintz (*Sefer ha-Histalkut*) has compiled an anthology of accounts of the death of various saints, from the *Ari* to the Baal Shem Tov to the present day. Naturally, most of the material is legendary. The following relies heavily on Mintz.

THE ARI

When the Ari (Isaac Luria) was on his deathbed, he told his disciples that after his death, he would return to earth to teach them. They asked him how such a thing could be possible. He replied that it was not for them to inquire into such matters; he might return to them in a dream, or in a vision while they were still awake. He then said to R. Isaac ha-Kohen, "Leave at once, for you are a *kohen.*" Isaac had no sooner left the house when the master opened his mouth and his soul departed with a kiss.[2]

THE BAAL SHEM TOV

The Baal Shem Tov died on the first day of Shavuot. He had been suffering from diarrhea since Passover, but he had not told his disciples of his malady. Shortly before he died, he explained how the soul emanates from this member of the body and from that member. Instructing his disciples to pray, he declared, "I shall be with you." A servant overheard the master saying, "Do not forsake me," and the master explained that he had been addressing the angel of death, who used to run away from him. He gave the disciples a sign that at the moment of his passing, the clocks would stop. Indeed, after he had gone to the toilet and then washed his hands, the large clock stopped. He gestured for his disciples to surround him, and he recited Torah to them. He then lay down and rose up again several times. He gradually became quiet, and then the smaller clock stopped. They put a feather under his nose and then realized that he had died.[3]

GERSHON HENOCH LEINER OF RADZHYN

This final example from Mintz typifies the hasidic emphasis.[4] The saintly hero of this story is R. Gershon Henoch Leiner of Radzhyn (d. 1891).

> A few weeks before R. Gershon Henoch became ill, he spoke much about death, saying that one should not be afraid of death and so forth. When the illness became severe and he was obliged to take to his bed, he secluded himself first in his private room, and he was overheard reciting the verses in Psalms, "Do I not hate them, O Lord, that hate Thee? . . . And lead me in the way everlasting" (Psalm 139:21–24), and he then took to his bed. When the illness became very severe and he was in great pain, he still uttered not a single groan. They asked him, "Why do you not ease your pain by groaning a little?"
>
> He replied, "One who has complaints against God groans, but one who has no complaints suffers everything in silence, accepting his sufferings in love."

NAHMAN OF BRATZLAV

R. Nahman of Bratzlav, great-grandson of the Baal Shem Tov, died of tuberculosis at the early age of 38. The deathbed scene is described by his disciple and biographer, Nathan of Nemirov.[5] Whenever R. Nahman wished to engage in deep contemplation, he would roll a ball of wax in his fingers to assist his concentration. Even in his last hours, writes Nathan, he continued to roll his ball of wax, and he remained completely lucid. As the end was fast approaching, those present recited the special prayer for the departure of saints (*tzaddikim*). Nathan continues:

It was not long before he passed away and was gathered unto his fathers in great sanctity and purity. Bright and clear, he passed away without any confusion whatsoever, without a single untoward gesture, in a state of awesome calm. Many members of the burial society were there, and all said that while they had observed many people passing away with clarity of mind, they had never before witnessed anything like this.

SHNEUR ZALMAN OF LIADY

The sons of R. Shneur Zalman of Liady, in their introduction to his *Shulhan Arukh,* are somewhat circumspect in describing their father's death. In later hasidic lore, however, the account is elaborated in the hagiographical spirit.[6] Just before he died, it is reported in the later account, the master took his pen and began to compose the essay beginning with the words "The soul that is truly humble . . ." He then asked his grandson, "Do you see the beam on the ceiling?" The grandson did not understand the question, but the master said, "Believe me, I do not see it. I see only the Divine energy by which every material object is sustained. Apart from this I see nothing." Then the master departed to the Source of life.

THE GAON OF VILNA

The Lithuanian-mitnaggedic school has its own tales of the demise of the saints. Landau, drawing on earlier accounts, tells this story about the death of the Gaon of Vilna.[7] The Gaon had been refusing medical care, but his sons, witnessing his distress, eventually summoned Dr. Lubashitz to his bedside. The doctor, bending down to hear what the saint was trying to say, heard him reciting from memory a section of the Mishnah. Until the very end the Gaon's mind was on his studies. The Gaon's disciples explained that he was busy preparing the lecture he would be called upon to deliver in the Garden of Eden. As he was about to die, the Gaon took hold of his *tzitzit,* saying, "How hard is it to depart from this world, where, for a few kopeks, a man can purchase *tzitzit* and thereby reach such an elevated stage as to meet with the *Shekhinah.* Where can one find anything like this in the world of souls, even if one gave all one's strength over it?" Having said this, he departed this life.

THE HAZON ISH

Abraham Isaiah Karelitz (1878–1953), the *Hazon Ish,* was a contemporary charismatic leader of the Lithuanian school. The account of his death is more subdued and more factual than such stories usually are.[8] On the last Friday night of his life, the *Hazon Ish* ate his Sabbath meal, after which he took his usual Sabbath walk, accompanied by a student at the Slabodka Yeshivah. He then went to the house of study to examine a book. At midnight he went to sleep. Awakening later in pain, he took his pills with a little tea. He said to the student who was looking after him, "I feel very ill." The doctor was quickly summoned, but it was too late. The *Hazon Ish* had suffered a severe heart attack. This otherwise completely factual account ends with these words: "Then the heart of the Jewish people stopped beating without anyone being aware that it had happened. The pure wings that covered the poor, anguished generation were gathered in."

YEHIEL M. TYKOCHINSKY

A similarly factual account of the death of a member of the Lithuanian school is that of Rabbi Yehiel M. Tykochinsky (1872–1955).[9] However, this story is not without a mystical cast. The account, written by the rabbi's son, is appended to the rabbi's *Gesher ha-Hayyim* (Bridge of Life), a compendium on the laws of death and mourning. As the rabbi was about to die, fully conscious of what was happening, the doctor gently hinted that since the end was very near, he should recite the *Adon Olam* hymn. The rabbi smiled softly and said, "I know what I have to say." Then, pointing to a chair, he repeated, "My teacher, Reb Samuel, my teacher, Reb Samuel," indicating that his teacher had come to escort him to the next world. Terror seized hold of those who heard these words. With great difficulty, the rabbi sipped some water so as to be able to recite the benediction over it. He then washed his hands in readiness to depart. He told those who were in attendance to open the windows and to rearrange the bed so that it would face the east. The rabbi was then overheard reciting the deathbed confession. The account concludes:

> At seven o'clock in the evening, on the eve of the eighth day of Nisan, my father's soul departed just as one takes off a garment in order to don another, while speaking words of Torah, in the presence of many *minyanim* of rabbis and heads of yeshivot, teachers, students, neighbors, friends, and relatives, with his face, shining with an ethereal light, turned towards the people. Our eyes witnessed the extinguishing of the pure candelabrum in which the lamps of Torah life had been daily kindled, burning for eighty-three years.

THE HATAM SOFER

Among the accounts from the Hungarian school is that of the death of R. Moshe Sofer, the *Hatam Sofer.*[10] On the first night of Sukkot, the rabbi's granddaughter, a little girl of 4, awoke crying bitterly. She had had a dream in which her beloved grandfather had died. Although the rabbi was alive and well, he indicated that he had had a premonition of his imminent death. Sometime after that, he fell ill during his prayers and was obliged to take to his bed. When someone tried to console him that the pain would go away and he would soon be restored to good health, he replied, "You are wrong. The gates of mercy have been closed." Although he was in great pain, he continued to teach the Torah from his bed. All the doctors failed to understand how the human mind could be capable of such lucidity in these circumstances.

The community heads visited the rabbi and asked him to designate his son as his successor in the rabbinate of Pressburg, and he complied. He then asked everyone to leave, explaining that he wished to rehearse all that he had studied in order to have his "learning in his hand" when he entered Paradise. Shortly thereafter, he forecast that he would die the next day at exactly half an hour after seven o'clock. He then prayed over the members of the community who had come to receive the master's last blessing.

In the morning he recited his prayers with a *minyan,* wearing the *tefillin* of Rashi and Rabbenu Tam, which he then presented to his faithful retainer, explaining that he would no longer need them, for the next day he would be in that state in which a man is exempt from keeping the *mitzvot.* He then asked those in attendance to give him an iced drink, and he was still sufficiently lucid to be able to discuss with them the precise benediction to be recited over it. Here the *kohen* motif recurs. He advised Rabbi Mordecai Katz to leave the house because the end was near.[11] He asked his students to study the Torah at his bedside, so that his soul should leave this world for the next attended by words of Torah. He then recited the *Shema* in a loud voice, the huge crowd outside reciting it after him. He then recited the *Shema* a second time. The third recitation was very soft, and his soul departed as he said "is One."

THE SAINTS AS MARTYRS

Accounts of the deaths of the martyrs are many. Those who gave their lives for their faith are called *kedoshim,* "holy ones," probably because the act of martyrdom is called *kiddush ha-shem* (sanctification of the Name). The various martyrologies composed during the Middle Ages extol the heroism of the martyrs who went to their death proclaiming the unity of God. By a kind of automatic consensus, the victims of the Nazi Holocaust are called *kedoshim.* The seven-volume *Eleh Ezkerah* describes the martyr's death of the rabbis and communal leaders who perished during the Holocaust.[12]

THE HILULA: CAUSE FOR CELEBRATION

Like the *hilula* of Rabbi Simeon, to which reference was made at the beginning of this chapter, the anniversary of the death of a hasidic *zaddik* is called by the hasidim the *zaddik's hilula.* Contrary to the rabbinic tradition, according to which the anniversary of a parent's death is an occasion for sadness (*Nedarim* 12a), the *hilula* of the saint is a celebration, because on each anniversary of his death, the saint's soul attains a more elevated state. R. Levi Yitzhak of Berditchev writes: "When the souls of the *tzaddikim* depart this world to enter the world of truth, they forget this lowly world, for they have entered a world of such delight that our minds cannot grasp it."[13] On the day of the *zaddik's yahrzeit,* the supplicatory prayers (*tahanun*) are not recited by the hasidim, as if the day were a festival. After the service, a toast is drunk to the saint's memory.[14] Reuben Margaliot published his *Hilula de-Tzaddikaya,* a list of the dates of the *yahrzeit* of famous *zaddikim* for this purpose and for the purpose of visiting the graves of the *zaddikim.*[15] Margaliot adds, however, that *tahanun* should not be omitted. Margaliot's book also records the anniversaries of famous non-hasidic or pre-hasidic saints.

THE SAINT AS JUDGE ON HIGH

There developed, especially in Hasidism, the notion that the departed saints become members of the Court on High, which judges other departed souls or pronounces judgment on people still alive on earth. Israel Klepholtz has published a volume of tales about the participation of the zaddikim in the activities of the Court on High.[16] The idea of the saints participating in the judgment in Paradise is also found in the literature and folklore of both Christianity and Islam.

10

VENERATION OF THE SAINTS

Since talmudic times, renowned saintly figures have been treated with veneration, as is evidenced by the numerous tales of the lives of the saints contained in the Talmud.[1] The term *tzaddik* in the Talmud generally refers simply to a good man; it was not until the Beshtian reinterpretation that the word came to be used in reference to the saint.[2] Occasionally, however, the *tzaddik* in the Talmud is a renowned saint, as in the saying (*Sanhedrin* 65b) that the *tzaddikim,* if they are free of sin, are capable of creating the world.[3] In the same passage there is an account of a saint creating a man.[4] In another talmudic passage (*Yoma* 38b) it is said that the whole world was created for the sake of a single *zaddik.*[5] The kabbalists applied the implications of these passages to the great masters of the Kabbalah, especially R. Simeon b. Yohai, the supposed author of the Zohar, and Isaac Luria, the Ari. In Hasidism, on the other hand, they were applied to the hasidic *zaddik.*

On *Lag ba-Omer,* to this day, the mystical devotees dance around bonfires while singing *Bar Yohai,* a song in honor of the great master composed by the sixteenth-century kabbalist Simeon Labi.[6] In English translation, the refrain of this song reads, "Happy art thou, Bar Yohai. Thou hast been anointed with the oil of gladness above thy fellows" (based on Psalm 45:8). The final stanza reads, "Bar Yohai, happy is she who gave birth to thee, happy the people who study thee [for example, thy work, the Zohar]. And happy are those who grasp thy secret, who wear the breastplate containing thine *Urim ve-Tumim.*"

CLEAVING TO THE SAGES

In Hasidism, the *zaddik* is venerated as a spiritual guide and mentor. On the verse "But ye that did cleave (*ha-devekim*) unto the Lord your God are alive every one of you this day" (Deuteronomy 4:4), the talmudic rabbis ask, "Is it possible to cleave to the *Shekhinah,* concerning whom it is written, 'For the Lord thy God is a devouring fire' (Deuteronomy 4:24)? But the meaning is, Any man who marries his daughter to a scholar (*talmid hakham*) or carries on a trade on behalf of scholars or benefits scholars from his estate is regarded by Scripture as if he had cleaved to the *Shekhinah*" (*Ketubot* 111b).

Maimonides (*Yad, Deot* 6:2) formulates this as follows: "It is a positive precept to cleave to the sages and their disciples in order to learn from their ways, as it is said, 'And to Him shalt thou cleave' (*u-vo tidbak,* Deuteronomy 10:20). Is it possible for a man to cleave to the *Shekhinah?* But the sages explain the precept to mean 'Cleave to the sages and their disciples.' "

Similarly, Aaron ha-Levi of Barcelona writes: " 'And to Him shalt thou cleave.' This means that we are commanded to cleave to the sages learned in the Torah so as to learn from them her glorious precepts and they will teach us the true ideas contained therein, of which they have a reliable tradition."[7] In all this there is an explicit denial that one can cleave to God; rather, one can cleave only to His Torah and to the sages who teach it. In Beshtian Hasidism, however, the ideal of *devekut* does mean attachment to God (that is, the mind should be centered on God at all times). But since such an ideal is beyond the reach of the ordinary *hasid,* he should cleave to his mentor, the *zaddik*, through association with whom a degree of *devekut* will be possible for him as well. The sages and scholars referred to in the talmudic passages are now the *zaddikim.* Many a hasidic text stresses that the ideal of *devekut* requires attachment to a master to whom one owes allegiance.

Mordecai Blum, a Jerusalem follower of R. Aaron Roth (1894–1944), recently published an anthology of hasidic teachings on the high duty of choosing a rebbe. The book has the revealing title *U-Vo Tidbak,* "And to Him Shalt Thou Cleave," where the reference is no longer to the sages, but to the *zaddikim*. The chapters of this book include "Faith in *Zaddikim,*" "Journeying to *Zaddikim,*" "Rules regarding Faith in Sages," "Becoming Bound to *Zaddikim,*" "Loving *Zaddikim* and Associates," "The Deeds of the *Zaddikim,*" "The Ways in which the *Zaddikim* Worship God" and "Their Eating, and the *Shirayyim* of the *Zaddik.*" The latter title refers to the hasidic practice of eating the food that the *zaddik* had first tasted at the sacred meal (*shirayyim,* "remainders").[8]

TELLING THE TALES

To tell of the *zaddik's* mode of worship, the miracles he has performed, the help he has offered to those in distress, was considered in Hasidism to be of the highest religious value.[9] It was believed not only that the tales were helpful in promoting ethical and spiritual values, but that the mere telling of the tales could succeed in bringing blessing and prosperity down from on high. Through the reliving of the tales, the original spiritual energy of the *zaddik* is once again released for the benefit of the narrators (usually the more venerable *hasidim*) and their audience. In one of the numerous collections of such tales, H. J. Moskovitch remarks that *hasidim* are wont to say that it is especially advantageous to relate tales of three *zaddikim* after the Sabbath.[10] Tales about the Baal Shem Tov are good "for children" (for being blessed with offspring). Tales about R. Elimelech of Lizensk are good for life (for health). Tales of Elimelech's brother, Susya, are good for sustenance (earning a living). But R. Israel of Ruzhany is said to have added that it is a *mitzvah* to tell these tales not only after the Sabbath but at all times, and not only of these three but of all the *zaddikim,* and not only for the three things stated but for all blessings, material or spiritual. In *Shivhey ha-Besht* (In praise of the Baal Shem Tov), it is said that when one tells the tales of the *zaddikim,* it is as if one were engaged in *Maaseh Merkavah.*[11] Joseph Perl's anti-hasidic satire *Megalleh Temirin* contains a number of references from early hasidic writings in which it is stated that to tell tales of the *zaddikim* is of a very high religious order.[12]

Many of the *hasidim* were not unaware of the element of sheer gullibility in the hasidic tale. For instance, in a letter of approbation to a collection of tales on the miraculous birth of the *zaddikim,* R. Joseph Schwartz of Grosswardein, after quoting from hasidic works on the advantage of telling such tales, remarks, "However, when engaged in this activity one must be very careful not to refer to matters that do no more than invite mockery. So I assume you will exercise due caution and publish only tales that come from a reliable source."[13] Schwartz quotes the Munkacser Rebbe Hayyim Eleazar Schapira, who remarks that nowadays people oppose the Torah and publish downright lies.[14]

WORSHIP AND NECROMANCY

The veneration of the *zaddikim* that at times bordered on worship, or, at least, on the view that the *zaddik* was an intermediary between God and man, was one of the chief complaints against the hasidim. Compared with his master, the Vilna Gaon, R. Hayyim of Volozhyn (1740–1821) was a more moderate critic of Hasidism. R. Hayyim's *Nefesh ha-Hayyim* was first published in Vilna in 1824, by which time the fury of the debate between the *hasidim* and the *mitnaggedim* had abated to some extent. The *Nefesh ha-Hayyim* is largely a theology of traditional rabbinism. In the process there is an implicit critique of some aspects of Hasidism, although R. Hayyim does not mention by name those whose views he is attacking. On the question of veneration for the holy man, R. Hayyim remarks:[15]

> Even to become subordinate and attached (*le-hitdabbek*) in some manner of worship to the holy spirit in some man, prophet, or inspired person is also called idolatry. We find that Nebuchadnezzar bowed down to Daniel not because he imagined Daniel to be God, Creator of all, but his intention, when he bowed down to him, was to become subordinate and attached to the holy spirit that was in him. Yet the rabbis (*Sanhedrin* 93a) call it idolatry even though the king's intention was only to worship the holy spirit that was in him.[16]

Especially among Oriental Jews and the hasidim, pilgrimages to the graves of the saints were, and still are, made. Goldziher has shown how Islamic folk beliefs tended to reinterpret the sites of pagan worship so that they came to be places in which saints are buried and hence became sacred spots.[17] It is ironic that graves of Islamic saints were similarly reidentified by Oriental Jews as being the last resting place of Jewish saints, to be visited for prayer and supplication–not, of course, for prayers to the saints themselves, but for prayers that the saints should intercede on behalf of the visitors.[18]

The whole question of intercession at the graves of the saints exercised the minds of the traditional halakhists. The main discussion centers on two talmudic passages. In one (*Sotah* 34b), it is said that Caleb prostrated himself on the graves of the patriarchs and said to them, "My fathers, pray on my behalf that I may be delivered from the plot of the spies." In the other passage (*Taanit* 47a), it is said that on days of fasting people go out to the graves to ask the dead to pray on their behalf. Against this is the prohibition of necromancy (Deuteronomy 18:11). The general line adopted by the majority of the halakhists is that since the saints are asked only to pray on behalf of the supplicants, the question of necromancy does not arise.[19] The Zohar (III, 71a–71b), in fact, goes so far as to say that "inquiring of the dead" does not apply to the saints, since they are still alive.[20]

The pilgrimage on *Lag ba-Omer* to the Meron tomb of R. Simeon b. Yohai, still exceedingly popular among kabbalists, Oriental Jews, and hasidim, was similarly viewed with suspicion by the traditional halakhists because of some of the practices engaged in there, such as burning costly garments in the saint's honor.[21] Far from the opposition discouraging the pilgrimage, similar pilgrimages are increasingly made to the graves of other saints, such as that of Rabbi Meir at Tiberias. On a visit to Jerusalem some years ago, I saw a poster advertising a bus trip to the grave of Jonathan b. Uziel. The poster advised bachelors in particular to make the journey, since "it is well known how efficacious it is for those who wish to make a good match." Mausoleums built over the tombs of hasidic saints have long been a pilgrimage destination; followers even deposit petitions there for the saint to pray on their behalf as he did while on earth.

R. Hayyim ha-Kohen makes an interesting statement in this

connection, that although he was a priest, forbidden to come into contact with a corpse or a grave, he would have touched the corpse of Rabbenu Tam (d. 1171), had he been present when the great teacher died, since the bodies of the saints do not contaminate.[22] This, too, was a source of much halakhic discussion, with the majority of the halakhists arguing that it is not permissible for a *kohen* to come into contact with the corpse or grave of even a renowned saint.[23] Rabbenu Tam and R. Hayyim ha-Kohen lived in Christian France. Is there any influence here of the Christian cult of the saints?[24]

JUDAISM DOES KNOW OF SAINTS

We have examined throughout this book the phenomenon of saintliness as it appears in Judaism, and, in the process, given the lie to the absurd suggestion that Judaism is too matter-of-fact to have room in its theology for Heaven-stormers who count the world well lost in their attempt to come closer to God. I have described both the values and some of the less admirable features of saintliness and hope that my research will be of interest to believer and nonbeliever, to Jew, Christian, and Muslim, and to the general reader as well as the academic. Yet I cannot bring this book to a close without expressing the hope that the tale I have told will be a little more than an investigation into personalities and events belonging solely to the past. The religious believer may possibly be stimulated to consider afresh how some of the material presented here can help in his or her own spiritual quest.

NOTES

CHAPTER 1

1. See Cohn, "Sainthood," for a brief sketch of our theme and for a discussion of whether the term *saint,* taken from Christianity, can be applied to the holy adherents of other religions.
2. This first part of the chapter draws on my article "The Concept . . ."; see also ET, vol. 16, s.v. *hasid,* pp. 385–389.
3. Gulkovitsch, *Die Entwicklung.*
4. Gulkovitsch, *Die Bildung.*
5. Greenstone, p. 159.
6. See *BDB* s.v. *hasad.*
7. S. L. Brown, pp. 47–49.
8. *Studies,* vol. 2, p. 151.
9. Cf. *Sifre,* Deuteronomy 49: "Just as the Holy One, blessed be He, is called a *hasid,* be thou a *hasid.*"
10. Gulkovitsch; *Die Entwicklung,* p. 11, n. 1.
11. Gulkovitsch, *Die Entwicklung,* pp. 18f.
12. Pages 13–14.
13. Pages 151–152.
14. Schürer, vol. 2, pp. 555–561; Oesterley, pp. 256–257.
15. Büchler, p. 8 n. 2.
16. See my "How much . . ."
17. See S. B. Urbach, pp. 87–196; Husik, pp. 80–113.
18. See Shrock.

19. Schechter, *Studies,* vol. 3, pp. 1–24.
20. For Judah the Saint, see Aptowitzer, pp. 343–350; on *Hasidey Ashkenaz,* see Zinberg, vol. 2, Chapters 3 and 4, pp. 35–76 and pp. 237–238; Markus, "The Devotional Ideals."
21. Ed. Lange.
22. See EJ, vol. 7, pp. 1388–1390. The *Sefer Hasidim* was published in two distinct versions: (1) Bologna, in 1538, the ed. on which Margaliot's is based; and (2) the Parma ms., used as a basis for the Wistinetzki ed.
23. See, e.g., in the Margaliot ed., nos. 197, 206, 212, 221, 222, 299, 697.
24. See Trachtenberg for the superstitions.
25. Zinberg, p. 46.
26. For the resemblances as well as the differences between the *Hasidey Ashkenaz* and the Kabbalah, which also reached its zenith in the thirteenth century, see Dan, *The Early Kabbalah,* pp. 18–23.
27. See Cronbach.
28. Ed. Wistinetzki, nos. 877–928, pp. 215–229.
29. See Scholem, *Major Trends,* pp. 104f.
30. "Religious Social Tendency."
31. Zinberg, p. 71, n. 42 states that this section in the *Rokeah* is paralleled to a large extent in *Sefer Hasidim,* ed. Margaliot, no. 7.
32. Schechter, *Studies,* vol. 2, pp. 202–306.
33. See EJ, vol. 3, pp. 834–835.
34. *Shem ha-Gedolim,* vol. 1, no. 42.
35. For the influence of Ibn Attar on Beshtian Hasidism, see Bakan, pp. 44a–50b.
36. The translation is Kaplan's except for one or two small changes.
37. *Students, Scholars,* p. 125.
38. *Cf.* Bloch: *Ruah Eliyahu,* p. 5, who states that from the year 1750, when the Gaon was 30 years old, he was called "the *hasid* of Vilna" by everyone because of the extreme sanctity of his life.
39. On Israel Salanter, see the book with this title by Goldberg.
40. Scholem, *Major Trends,* p. 118.
41. See Nahshuni for full details and Plaut, Introduction, pp. 1–5.
42. Nahshuni, p. 38.

43. On Adler, see Avneri and Sofer, *Hut ha-Meshulash,* pp. 16–20; Schwartz, *Derekh ha-Nesher;* Dubnow, *Toledot,* pp. 434–441.
44. Dubnow, op. cit.
45. Op. cit. p. 441.
46. Sofer, *Hut ha-Meshulash,* p. 20.
47. The chapter in Nahshuni about the relationship between the *Hatam Sofer* and Hasidism, pp. 232–252.
48. See Rafaeli and A. Levi, *Derekh Tzaddikim.*
49. See Alfasi, *Baba Sali.*
50. See A. Levi, on the life of Yosef Sholomo Dayyan.

CHAPTER 2

1. *Major Trends,* pp. 80–118.
2. Page 91.
3. Commentary to Exodus 18:25.
4. Pages 62–63.
5. *Varieties,* p. 340.
6. Ed. Liebermann, pp. 36–38.
7. Preface, pp. 5–6.
8. Jacobs, *Hasidic Prayer,* pp. 17–21.
9. Wilensky, Index, s.v. *bittul Torah u-vizayon lomedeha.*
10. *Cf.* Joseph Weiss, "Torah Study in Early Hasidism," in his *Studies,* pp. 56–68.
11. See Lamm for a full discussion of this topic.
12. *Yosher Divrey emet,* vol. 1, no. 22, p. 122.
13. *Yosher Divrey Emet,* vol. 1, no. 8, p. 113.
14. *Raza de-Uvda,* Preface, p. 9.
15. Katz, *Pulmus.*

CHAPTER 3

1. *Major Trends,* pp. 15–16.
2. See Jacobs, *Jewish Mystical Testimonies.*

3. No. 38, ed. Wistinetzki p. 40.
4. *The Esoteric Philosophy,* p. 37.
5. No. 43, ed. Wistinetzki, p. 41.
6. No. 119, ed. Wistinetzki, pp. 59–60.
7. No. 120, ed. Wistinetzki, p. 60.
8. No. 127, ed. Wistinetzki, p. 61.
9. No. 577, ed. Wistinetzki, p. 241.
10. No. 1661, ed. Wistinetzki, p. 402.
11. No. 1946, ed. Wistinetzki, pp. 470–471.
12. *Sefer Raziel,* pp. 96–100; see Jacobs, *Jewish Mystical Testimonies,* pp. 48–55.
13. See Fine, *Safed Spirituality,* pp. 83–156.
14. Chapters 18–21.
15. *Va-yetze,* pp. 40–41.
16. Ed. Koretz, 1770, p. 23a.
17. *Derekh Pikkudekha, mitzvot aseh,* no. 41:11–12, p. 175.
18. *Ohev Yisrael, Likkutim va-yikra,* beg. pp. 278–279.
19. *Avodat Yisrael, shemini,* end, p. 50a.

CHAPTER 4

1. Pages 302–331.
2. Pages 339–340.
3. A good example of this approach is Abba Hillel Silver's *Where Judaism Differed.*
4. Vol. 1, pp. 137–138.
5. The source is *The Letters of the Hafetz Hayyim* (Heb.) in the *Collected Works,* published by Friedman (New York) 1952, section on the saint's conduct in vol. 1, no. 68, pp. 37–38.
6. In R. Hayyim's introduction to the Gaon's commentary to the *Sifra de-Tzeniuta,* end, p. 6b. *Cf.* Aaron ha-Levi of Barcelona, *Sefer ha-Hinnukh, mitzvah* 270, *emor,* that the Torah does not permit the High Priest to come into contact with his near relatives when they die, because in his attachment to God he was separated from his relatives even while they were alive.

7. From Alexander Süsskind's Ethical Will, no. 43, printed at end of his *Yesod ve-Shoresh ha-Avodah,* pp. 488–489.
8. On R. Yoizel Horowitz see Katz, *Tenuat ha-Musar,* vol. 4, pp. 179–351, and *Pulmos ha-Musar,* pp. 25–31.
9. *Noam Elimelekh,* ed. Nigal, vol. 2, pp. 614–618.
10. Based on *Tikkuney Zohar,* nos. 21 and 58.
11. *Otzar ha-Hayyim: Minhagey Tzanz,* by J. D. Weissberg, pp. 4–5.
12. D. Werner, *Tzaddik Yesod Olam,* vol. 1, pp. 159–179.
13. Vol. 1, pp. 237–269, in the 3-vol. ed.
14. Kahana, *Bet Shelomo,* nos. 125–126, pp. 47b–48a; no. 98, pp. 42a–42b; no. 97, pp. 41a–41b; no. 122, pp. 47a–47b; nos. 130–131, p. 48b.
15. Fine, *Safed Spirituality,* pp. 47–53.
16. Fine, *op. cit.,* p. 42.
17. For this legend about R. Joseph's blindness, see *Tanhuma,* ed. Buber, *hukkat,* p. 66a; Nahmanides (*Ramban*) to *Kiddushin* 31a; *Ran* to *Rif, Kiddushin* 13a in the Vilna ed.; *Seder ha-Dorot,* Amoraim, s.v. *R. Yosef;* Urbach; *Hazal,* p. 67, n. 97.

CHAPTER 5

1. See Scholem, *Major Trends,* pp. 96–97, on the ideal of equanimity in Jewish mysticism, remarking on the origin of the ideal among the Stoics and Cynics and its later development in early Christian thought and among the Sufis.
2. For the influence of Sufism on Bahya, see EJ, vol. 15, pp. 486–487.
3. Ed. Liebermann, vol. 2, p. 9.
4. For this doctrine in Hasidism, see Jacobs, *Seeker of Unity,* s.v. *annihilation of self.*
5. Part 5, *Shaar Yihud ha-Maaseh,* Chapter 2, in ed. Liebermann, vol. 2, p. 9.
6. Part 5, *ibid.,* Chapter 5, Liebermann, pp. 35–36.
7. Ed. Erlanger, *ekev,* pp. 281–282. Scholem, *op. cit.,* n. 59 on p. 372, quotes the source as Jellinek's *Beitrage,* but since then the book has appeared in print in this Erlanger ed. On Isaac of Acre, see EJ, vol. 9, pp. 29–30.
8. See the famous essay of Scholem, "*Devekut,* or Communion with God," in his *The Messianic Idea,* pp. 203–227.

9. I have been unable to discover the identity of this Rabbi Abner.
10. *Reshit Hokhma ha-Shalem,* ed. Waldman, *shaar ha-Ahavah* 3:30 (vol. 1, pp. 398–399).
11. *Shaarey Kedushah,* Part 3, Chapter 4, p. 25b.
12. *Shiflut,* as used here, is as a key expression in hasidic literature.
13. See Rivkah Schatz Uffenheimer, *Quietistic Elements,* p. 153, n. 18, that the derivation of the doctrine from the verse in Psalms is found only in the Maggid, not in anything attributed to the Baal Shem Tov himself. See, however, Dunner, *Mayyim Rabbim,* p. 118, to Psalm 16, where, attributed to Yehiel Michal of Zlotchow, the verse is understood as referring to *hishtavut,* not in the sense of relationship to other human beings, but to God (i.e., it is all the same whether God visits a man with suffering or treats him with mercy). *Cf.* the interpretation of "Even if everyone says you are righteous be in your own eyes as if you are wicked" (*Niddah* 30b; i.e., it should be all the same to you), see Jacob Joseph of Pulnoyye, *Toledot, shelah* (p. 524, no. 10) in name of R. Laib Pustiner. *Cf.* the references to *hishtavut* in *Amud ha-Avodah* by R. Baruch of Kossov (d. 1795), Tchernowiotz, 1863, pp. 145a–145b, quoting the passage in Bahya, referred to by Piekarz, *Biymey Tzemihat ha-Hasidut,* pp. 119–120.
14. *Or Torah* to Psalm 16:8, no. 179; *Tzavaat ha-Ribash,* no. 2, p. 1.
15. Schatz Uffenheimer, *op. cit., loc. cit.,* discusses whether the *people* to whom the Maggid refers are people in general or the *Mitnaggedim.* If the latter, then this passage is part of the hasidic polemics in defense of their views. It seems probable that the Maggid is thinking of people in general, since he seems to be advocating the ideal of equanimity.
16. For the "holy sparks" idea in Hasidism, see Jacobs, *Hasidic Thought,* pp. 170–173, and essay in Green, *Jewish Spirituality,* vol. 2, pp. 99–126.
17. *Darkhey Yesharim,* no actual pagination, but it is on p. 4b.
18. See the version in *Likkutey Amarim,* Lemberg, 1911, p. 29b. The publishers attribute this work to Menahem Mendel of Vitebsk (1730–1788), but it is odd that the saying should appear in more or less the same words in both works. There seems to be confusion between the two Menahem Mendels. In this version the reading is not "such an attitude brings about attachment," but "attachment brings about this attitude."
19. See Berger, *Eser Orot,* no. 42, p. 94, from *Tefillah le-Moshe,* by Moses of Sambur.
20. See Guttmann, *Rabbi Dov mi-Leova,* no. 48, p. 29. For the equanimity ideal

in a non-Hasidic work, see Alexander Süsskind of Grodno (d. 1794), *Yesod ve-Shoresh ha-Avodah,* pp. 31–33, quoted as a very close parallel to the passage in *Tzavaat ha-Ribash,* by Piekarz, *op. cit.,* pp. 373–375. Piekarz discusses the relationship between these two texts.

CHAPTER 6

1. *The Mystical Experience in Abraham Abulafia.* See especially Idel's comparison of Abulafia's mysticism with the approach of the *Hasidey Ashkenaz.*
2. Idel has a chapter titled "Erotic Images for the Ecstatic Experience," pp. 179–228. This topic is considered at the end of this chapter.
3. *Religion in Essence and Manifestation,* p. 490.
4. *Midrash Pinhas,* no. 34, p. 7b.
5. *Sippurim Noraim,* pp. 27b–28a.
6. Kaddish, *Tiferet ha-Yehudi,* no. 140, p. 29b.
7. On *madregot,* see sup. pp. 41–45.
8. *be-Labbat Esh,* vol. 1, pp. 50–51.
9. See Nahshuni, *Rabbenu Moshe Sofer,* p. 237, for a report of a trance state experienced by this non-hasidic rabbinic figure.
10. Moskovitch, *Otzar,* Part 8, no. 2.
11. Rafaeli, *ha-Rav Sharabi,* pp. 100–101.
12. *Darkhey Tzedek,* no. 4, p. 2a. On these maxims see Gries, "The Sources and Editing," who detects three distinct strands: (1) from the school of the Maggid of Mesirech, (2) from the school of R. Jacob Joseph of Pulnoyye, (3) Menahem Mendel's own maxims.
13. *Darkhey Tzedek,* no. 17, p. 4b.
14. *Darkhey Tzedek,* no. 31, p. 5b.
15. *Darkhey Tzedek,* no. 33, p. 6a.
16. *Darkhey Tzedek,* no. 75, p. 10a.
17. *The Messianic Idea,* pp. 203–227.
18. Commentary to the Pentateuch, ed. Chavel, p. 398.
19. *The Messianic Idea,* p. 207.
20. I have been unable to locate this passage.

21. Scholem states that he had the good fortune to discover the manuscript to which Azikri refers.
22. *Mesillat Yesharim,* Chapter 26, ed. Kaplan, pp. 221–228.
23. Midrash Genesis Rabbah 82:6.
24. *Sidra, aharey mot,* p. 90.
25. This passage is in all probability the source of Zechariah Mendel of Yaroslav, see sup. pp. 70–71. In fact, R. Zechariah Mendel uses the very same words as *Or ha-Hayyim.*
26. *Ner la-Maor,* p. 10. In his biography of Attar in Bakan, *Yad Or ha-Hayyim,* Margaliot, p. 31, n. 36, remarks that this passage is deliberately written in riddle form.
27. *Or ha-Hayyim* to Deuteronomy 6:5, p. 384.
28. *Or ha-Hayyim,* p. 385.
29. *Major Trends,* Chapter 3, pp. 80–118.
30. *Sefer Raziel,* pp. 9b–10a; for the whole passage, see sup. pp. 36–37.
31. For a much shorter version, see the *Rokeah* beg. *Hilkhot Hasidut, shoresh ahavah,* pp. 6a–6b, see sup. p. 15.
32. *Yad, Teshuvah* 10:3.
33. *Or ha-Hayyim* to Deuteronomy 6:5, pp. 385–386.

CHAPTER 7

1. All the articles of Gries are extremely important for the history of the *hanhagot.*
2. Ed. Jerusalem, 1964, pp. 125–144.
3. Ed. Halevi, pp. 18b–19a.
4. Incorrectly given as letter 44. It is letter 45. See Y. Rafaeli's ed. of *Sefer ha-Manhig,* Jer., 1978, vol. 1, p. 84, and Rafaeli's n. 12.
5. See sup. p. 57 and p. 131n. 17.
6. *Studies in Judaism,* vol. 2, pp. 202 ff.
7. *Safed Spirituality,* pp. 27–80.
8. Fine, op. cit., pp. 34–38.
9. Ed. Munkacs, 1940 and var. eds.

10. On the Sharabi circle, see Jacobs, *Jewish Mystical Testimonies,* Chapter 14, pp. 156–175.
11. Ed. Amsterdam, 1712.
12. Gries has shown that all the early lists of hasidic *hanhagot* are only variants of the original list of the Maggid of Mesirech.
13. See the remarks of the *Shaarey Teshuvah* Responsum that the disciples of Rav were incapable of following all his rules.
14. *Tanya, Iggeret ha-Kodesh,* no. 25.
15. Sup. p. 53.
16. Introduction to his edition of *Noam Elimelekh,* pp. 16–18.
17. Sup. pp. 80–81.
18. Also in Weintraub, *Tzavvaot ve-hanhagot,* pp. 65–68, see Gries in *Zion* 46:4, pp. 280–281.
19. See M. N. Kohen on Kolbiel's notes.
20. Version 2 in Weintraub.
21. Also in many other places; e.g., in Klepholtz, *Torat ha-Maggid,* vol. 1, pp. 3–9.
22. Asher ha-Kohen, *Keter Rosh,* no. 13.
23. Pages 114–117.
24. Katz, op. cit., vol. 3, pp. 220–229.
25. Katz, op. cit., vol. 2, Chapter 16, pp. 172–192. Cf. the *hanhagot* of R. Yehial Michel Rabbinowitz (actual dates not given, but he was murdered by the Nazis ca. 1940) of the Lithuanian school; see biographical note in Weingarten's introduction to Rabbinowitz's *Afikey Yam* and I. Lewin's note in *Elleh Ezkarah,* vol. 4, 1966, pp. 76–80. Rabbinowitz's *hanhagot* are found in the Warsaw edition of *Afikey Yam,* end, under the heading *"Peniney Yam, Kunteros Aharon,"* pp. 5–6.
26. See Sofer, *Hut ha-Meshulash,* pp. 139–152; Feigenstock, pp. 47–57; Nahshuni, *Rabbenu Moshe Sofer,* pp. 437–450.
27. Feigenstock, pp. 56–57.

CHAPTER 8

1. See Malter, *Taanit,* pp. xx–xxi.
2. See the discussion by Loewe in Montefiore and Loewe, *A Rabbinic Anthology,* pp. 690–693.
3. See Jacobs, *A Jewish Theology,* pp. 115–124.

4. *Sippurey Hasidim,* p. 3.
5. *Hazal,* p. 92.
6. See "Jesus the Magician" in Encyclopedia Judaica, vol. 7, p. 171.
7. See Scholem, *Sabbatai Sevi,* pp. 605–606.
8. *Prayer Book,* p. 258, n.
9. Cf. Otto's analysis of the numinous in the Old Testament, pp. 72–81. For further talmudic statements on this theme, see *Berakhot* 19a, *Shabbat* 108a, *Moed Katan* 17a, *Hagigah* 3b, *Yevamot* 45a and 105b, *Nedarim* 50b, *Bava Kama* 117a, *Niddah* 36b, JT *Hagigah* 2:1(77a).
10. *Gedoley Hasidey Belz,* p. 36. On the idea that once the word has been spoken, see the talmudic references to Ecclesiastes 10:5, "like an error which precedeth from a ruler," in *Moed Katan* 18a, *Ketubot* 23a and 62b, *Bava Metzia* 68a, JT *Sotah* 9:15(24a), *Avodah Zarah* 2:2(44d).
11. *Od Yosef Hai,* p. 14.
12. *Pirkey Hayyim,* p. 98.
13. Cf. the story of the young couple who died as a result of having insulted R. Nathan Adler and his daughter in Sofer, *Hut ha-Meshulash,* pp. 23–24, and the stories under the heading *onesh* in Moskovitz, *Otzar,* Part 2, nos. 15 and 16, and Part 4, nos. 12–14, of people who suffered because they had offended the saints.
14. See Green, "Typologies."
15. See Jacobs, *Hasidic Prayer,* pp. 126–139, and Weiss, "The Great Maggid's . . ."
16. See sup. pp. 9–10
17. See, e.g., Levi Yitzhak of Berditchev, *Kedushat Levi, rosh ha-shanah,* p. 275.
18. See, e.g., Elimelech of Lizensk, *Noam Elimelekh* to Genesis 18:1, ed. G. Nigal, p. 43.
19. See, e.g., R. Jacob Joseph of Pulnoyye, *Ben Porat Yosef,* p. 80b; Green op. cit. p. 131; Dressner, *The Zaddik,* p. 277, n. 32, and p. 278, n. 34, where further examples are given from the writings of R. Jacob Joseph.
20. See, e.g., Moskovitz, *Maaseh Nehemiah,* p. 117.
21. See Green, op. cit., pp. 145–149. On the Seer of Lublin, see the fine article by Rachel Elior.
22. Moskovitz, *Otzar,* Part 5, no. 8.
23. For the literature on the pygmy on the giant's shoulders, see Haberman,

Maimonides and Aquinas, pp. 204–205. See the story of the Belzer Rebbe, R. Joshua, in Moskovitz, *Otzar,* Part 5, no. 8. The rebbe refused an invitation to become chief rabbi in New York because the United States was a new land, where the risk to the soul was great, unlike Europe, where the atmosphere had been purified through the deeds of the saints over many centuries. He advised those who were seeking a rabbi to go to Lithuania, where the great rabbis were unaware of the risk they would be taking by accepting a position in the United States.

24. Page 24a. Cf. Zohar I, 118a; III, 157b, on the same theme, quoted by Kalisch, *Kevod Hakhamim,* p. 10.
25. *Guide* III, 14.
26. See Lewin, *Otzar he-Geonim* to *Gittin* 68, pp. 152ff.
27. *Noam Elimelekh,* ed. G. Nigal, vol. 2, pp. 593–602.
28. *Noam Elimelekh, va-yeshev,* ed. G. Nigal, vol. 1, pp. 109–110.
29. *Midrash Pinhas,* p. 82, no. 7.
30. Section *Or Olam,* Chapter 1, no pagination.
31. *Eser Orot,* pp. 4–15. Moskovitz, *Maaseh Nehamiah,* no. 13, pp. 27–31, quotes Berger with some elaborations on the theme. On discovering new ideas in the Torah, see R. Shneur Zalman, *Tanya, Iggeret ha-Kodesh,* p. 145a, quoted by Kalisch op. cit., p. 9. On the question "Since the great saints of old prayed unsuccessfully for the Messiah to come, how can we pygmies hope for our prayers for his coming to be answered?" see *Seder ha-Yom ha-Katzar* at the beg. of *Sefer Niflaot Hadashot,* by Yehiel Moshe of Komarovka, p. 11. "Great builders are required to erect a building for its foundation to be strong, but to add to the building and complete it, men of lesser skills will do."
32. Rafaeli on Sharabi; Alfasi on Abuchatzeirah; Levi on Dayyan, Sharabi, and Savaani, see sup. p. 22.
33. Page 11.
34. Page 65. On the hasidic influence on the Oriental saints, see A. Levi, *Derekh Tzaddikim,* vol. 1, pp. 335–339, that Savaani regularly studied the classic hasidic work *Beer Mayyim Hayyim,* by Hayyim Tchernowitz, as well as the works of Nahman of Bratzlav.
35. Page 102.
36. Alfasi, pp. 49–50.
37. Pages 37–38.

38. Goldziher, pp. 269–270.
39. Pages 85–87. On the Yemenite saints Sharabi and Savaani, see A. Levi, *Derekh Tzaddikim* for the following:

    Vol. 1, pp. 245–246. A hasidic rebbe (name not supplied) asked Savaani to pray on behalf of his wife so that she would be blessed with a child. While waiting for the couple to arrive, the saint just happened to pick up a book in which it was stated that frequent visits by a woman to a cemetery prevent her having a child because of the unclean spirit there. Just at that moment the couple arrived, and apologized for being late, saying that they had made a pilgrimage to the grave of the *Hazon Ish.* Savaani advised the woman to cease visiting the cemetery, and the couple was soon blessed with a child.

    Vol. 1, p. 250. In his old age, Savaani was unable to make the journey to the tombs of the saints at Meron, Tiberias, and Safed. Nevertheless, he was able by means of special *yihudim* to be in contact with the souls of the departed saints, even in his own home. And, he remarked, Sharabi was able to do the same.

    Vol. 1, p. 254. Savaani used to bless people by placing his hand on the back of the suppliant's neck because it is there that sin is located. He would quote the verse "Thy hand shall be on the neck of thine enemies" (Genesis 49:8).

    Vol. 1, pp. 347–352. A curious story of how Sharabi and Savaani frustrated the designs of a miracle worker from London who was really a false Messiah.
40. See sup. pp. 73–75 and Bakan, *Yad Or ha-Hayyim,* pp. 20b–47a.
41. See Scholem article "Dibbuk." In the very early references to unclean spirits–e.g., in Josephus, *Antiquities* 8:2,5; Mark 8:1–20;3:22; Matthew 12:22, 44–45; Luke 11:16–25: Acts 19:13–15–the meaning is unclean spirits that invade the body of a living person. The concept of the *dybbuk* as a soul pursued by evil spirits that invades the body of a living person is very late, originating from the spread of the Lurianic Kabbalah and the Lurianic doctrine of reincarnation (*gilgul*).
42. The story is told in detail in Winkler, pp. 239–264.

CHAPTER 9

1. See supra, p. 73 on the death of Aaron's sons. For accounts of the death of the saints in JT, see *Avodah Zarah* 3:1(942c).
2. R. Hayyim Vital, *Sefer ha-Hezyonot,* p. 230b.

3. Ben-Amos, *In Praise,* no. 247, pp. 255–257.
4. Page 39; Mintz gives the source as *Dor Yesharim*(?)
5. Kaplan, *Rabbi Nachman's Wisdom,* pp. 444–445.
6. See Frumkin, *Shivhey ha-Rav* (no pagination, but toward the end of the book).
7. *Ha-Gaon he-Hasid mi-Vilna,* pp. 333–337.
8. Cohen, *Peer ha-Dor,* vol. 5, pp. 119–121.
9. *Gesher ha-Hayyim,* vol. 1, pp. 14–17.
10. Sofer, *Hut ha-Meshulash,* pp. 155–160.
11. See sup., p. 118.
12. On martyrdom, see Ben-Sasson, "Kiddush ha-Shem."
13. *Kedushat Levi, Likkutim Hadashim,* p. 532.
14. See Wertheim, *Haklakhot,* pp. 226–228.
15. See infra pp. 124–126.
16. See Klepholtz, *Sippurey Bet Din shel Maalah.*

CHAPTER 10

1. On the veneration of saints in religion generally, see Chapter 30, "Saints," in Van Der Leeuw, *Religion in Essence and Manifestation,* pp. 236–239.
2. See sup. pp. 19–20.
3. See Rashi ad loc.
4. This is the source of the Golem legend; see Scholem, *The Messianic Idea,* pp. 335–340.
5. Cf. *Berakhot* 6b, "The whole world was created for the sake of the God-fearing man."
6. S. Alexandri Sofer Schreiber.
7. *Sefer ha-Hinnukh,* no. 434.
8. On *shirayyim,* see Wertheim, *Halakhot,* pp. 167–169, and Hayyim Eleazar Shapira of Munkacs, *Divrey Torah,* vol. 1, no. 13, pp. 7–8. Tishby, "Zevi Hermann," p. 568, n. 66, remarks that no reference is made to the practice of *shirayyim* in the early anti-hasidic polemics, and there are only a very few references to it in hasidic literature. The question of when the practice was introduced into Hasidism has yet to be investigated.

9. See Wertheim, *Halakhot,* pp. 169–170. Cf. Dan, *The Hasidic Story,* that the *publication* of hasidic stories underwent the following development: (1) the parables told by the Baal Shem Tov and the early masters; (2) the *Shivhey ha-Besht* in 1815; (3) the tales of R. Nahman of Bratzlav, 1800–1811; (4) the praises of R. Nahman after his death; (5) The proliferation of Hasidic tales from 1865 to the First World War.
10. *Otzar ha-Sippurim,* p. 2.
11. Tale 194, p. 199.
12. Perl's remarks are to be found in his introduction, p. 1b, n. 11. Perl is hardly a reliable source, but the mere fact that much is made in his satire of relics of the saints, p. 52b, shows that the sale of relics must have been fairly widespread among the hasidim, otherwise Perl would not have built his plot around such sales. There are also later tales of rebbes blessing coins and the like for their followers to use as amulets, but for all that, relics play a very minor role in hasidic life.
13. Moskovitch, *Berakhah Meshuleshet,* beg. before p. 1.
14. *Divrey Torah,* Part 2, no. 78.
15. *Nefesh ha-Hayyim, Shaar* 3, chapter 10. Wilensky, vol. 2, pp. 345–349, quotes a number of implicit anti-Hasidic polemics in the *Nefesh has-Hayyim* but has overlooked this very important passage.
16. The notion of the thirty-six hidden saints is very late; see Scholem in EJ, vol. 10, pp. 1367–1368, and M. Beer, "Sources." It is based on the talmudic saying (*Sukkah* 45b) that there are never less than thirty-six zaddikim who receive the countenance of the *Shekhinah* (the beatific vision) each day. In Jewish folklore these became the *lamedvavniks*—the thirty-six *hidden* saints who appear to others as very ordinary, common folk but who are, in reality, great saints. It is noteworthy that the hasidic masters themselves do not belong in the ranks of the thirty-six, but there are tales of zaddikim who knew the identity of the *lamedvavniks.* For folk beliefs about men with miraculous powers, see Günzig.
17. Goldziher, pp. 281–286.
18. See Levi's biography of Yosef Sholomo Dayyan, *Od Yosef Hai,* chapter 5, pp. 65–102, for accounts of this contemporary saint visiting various tombs of the saints, especially that of the prophet Samuel, with whom he had regular conversations. Cf. Bilu's interesting study of the Moroccan saint David u-Moshe. Thousands of pilgrims visit this saint's tomb in the high Atlas mountains. But when many of his followers emigrated to

Israel, the saint's spirit was said to have taken up residence in Safed. See Bilu's essay for the extraordinary details.

19. See Encyclopedia Judaica, vol. 7, p. 247.
20. On the subject see Tykochinsky, *Gesher ha-Hayyim,* vol. 2, chapter 26, pp. 207–213.
21. See Sevin, *ha-Moadim ba-Halakhah,* vol. 2, pp. 360–364.
22. See Tosafists to *Ketubot* 103b, s.v. *oto ha-yom.*
23. See the survey by Langauer.
24. There are very few reports of Jewish saints having halos. Rashi (*Sanhedrin* 31b) quotes the legend of a saint around whose head a light shone. The Midrash (Exodus Rabbah 47) speaks of the rays of light that shone around the head of Moses. In *Sefer Hasidim,* ed. Margaliot, no. 370, there is a tale about a hasid with a halo around his head. See Scholem, *Kabbalah,* p. 188; Pietrekovsky, Part 3 n. on p. 268. Cf. Bahya, *shaar ahavat ha-shem,* Chapter 7.

GLOSSARY

Aliyat neshamah: ascent of the soul

Am ha-aretz: an ignorant person

Baaley shem: plural of baal shem, master of the divine Name – miracle worker

Baal madregah: one who has attained a high spiritual stage

Baal shem: master of the divine Name – miracle worker

Bishvil: in the path of

Bittul ha-yesh: annihilation of selfhood

Davuk: to be attached

Dayan: a judge

Devekut: attachment to God

Devekut gadol: attachment to God with intensity

Dybbuk: a soul of a dead person that has invaded a living body

Dybbukim: plural of dybbuk

Epikoros: unbeliever, heretic

Gadlut de-mohin: greatness of mind; elevation of soul

Gilgul: transmigration of the soul

Ha-hitdabbekut: the state of being in devekut

Hakham: a sage

Halakhot: laws, rules of conduct

Ha-mitbodedim: hermits

Hanhagah: rule of conduct

Hanhagot: plural of hanhagah

Hasadim: mercies, kindnesses

Hasid: a saint

Hasidah: feminine of hasid

Hasidim: plural of hasid

Hasidim ha-rishonim: the saints of olden times

Hasidism: eighteenth-century pietistic movement

Hasidut: saintliness

He-hasid: the saint

He-hasid she-bi-kehunah: the saint among the priests

hesed: loving kindness

Hilula: "marriage," the ascent of the soul at death

Hishtavut: equanimity

hitlahavut: enthusiasm

hitpashtut ha-gashmiyut: stripping off of corporeality, trance-like state

hokhmat ha-matzpun: wisdom of the conscience

Iggeret: letter

Ish hesed: kindly man

Kaddishin: holy ones (Aramaic)

Katnut de-mohin: smallness of mind, state of spiritual depression

Kedoshim: holy ones (Hebrew)

Kedushah: holiness, sanctification

Kelalim noraim: tremendous rules of conduct

Kiddush ha-Shem: martyrdom, lit. "sanctification of the divine Name"

Kohen: priest

Le-hitdabbek: to become attached to God or to a saint

Lishmah: for its own sake

Madregah: elevated stage of the soul

Madregot: plural of madregah

Marah shehorah: melancholy, lit. "black bile"

Maskilim: enlightened ones, advocates of Western culture

Matzah: unleavened bread eaten on Passover

Mazzal: luck

Merkavah: the Heavenly Chariot

Meturgeman: translator

Mikveh: ritual bath

Miley de-hasiduta: saintly matters

Minyan: quorum of ten for public prayer

Minyanim: plural of minyan, conventicles

Mishnat hasidim: a rule for saints

Mitat neshikah: death by a divine kiss

Mitzvah: a good deed

Nafal mi-madregato: fall from elevated state of soul

Nahat ruah: satisfaction

Nefilat ha-mohin: fall of the mind, spiritual depression

Nigleh: the revealed part of the Torah

Nistar: the esoteric part of the Torah

Perutah: a small coin; a cent or penny

Pirka: chapter, lecture

Rav: rabbi

Rebbe: Hasidic master

Ruah ha-kodesh: holy spirit, inspiration

Shaveh: equal

Shaveh etzlo: all the same to him

She-lo lishmah: not for its own sake, with an ulterior motive

Sheretz: a creeping thing, a rodent

Shevil: path; channel

Shiflut: humility

Shirayyim: remainder of food the saint has tasted

Tahanun: prayer of supplication

Tallit: prayer shawl

Talmid hakham: scholar

Tanna: Talmudic teacher of first two centuries C.E.

Tefillin: phylacteries

Tzaddik: saint, Hasidic master, righteous man

Tzaddikim: plural of tzaddik

Tzitzit: fringes

U-vo tidbak: 'and cleave to Him'

Yihud: unification, mystical trance

Yihudim: plural of yihud

Yoshevim: permanent residents in a Hasidic master's court

Zaddik: same as tzaddik, usual form of transliteration of tzaddik

REFERENCES

Aaron ha-Levi of Barcelona, *Sefer ha-Hinnukh,* var. eds.

Abelson, J., "Saints and Martyrs (Jewish)," in Encyclopedia of Religion, Macmillan, New York, vol. 11., pp. 62–63.

Abraham of Granada, *Berit Menuhah,* Warsaw, 1864.

Abraham Joshua Heschel of Apta, *Ohev Yisrael,* Jerusalem, 1962.

Abraham b. Nathan of Lunel, *Sefer ha-Manhig,* ed. Y. Rafael, Jerusalem, 1978.

Abraham of Sochachov, *Egley Tal,* New York, 1968.

Abrahams, Israel, *Jewish Ethical Wills,* 2nd ed., with foreword by Judah Goldin, Jewish Publication Society, Philadelphia, 1976.

Alexander Süsskind of Grodno, *Yesod ve-Shoresh ha-Avodah,* Jerusalem, 1965.

Alexandri, Sholomo Sofer Schreiber, *Shir Bar Yohai,* Jerusalem, n.d.

Alfasi, E., *Baba Sali,* biography of Israel Abuchatzeirah, Jerusalem, 1985; English trans. Leah Dolinger, New York, 1986.

Aptowitzer, V., *Mavo le-Sefer Ravia,* Jerusalem, 1938.

Asher ha-Kohen, *Keter Rosh* (*Orhot Hayyim*) in *Siddur Ishey Yisrael,* Tel-Aviv, 1968, pp. 521–544.

Attar, Hayyim, *Or ha-Hayyim,* var. eds., Jerusalem, n.d.

Avniri, Zvi, "Adler, Nathan," Encyclopedia Judaica, vol. 2, pp. 284–285.

Azikri, Eleazar, *Sefer Haredim,* Jerusalem, 1966.

Azuli, Hayyim Joseph David, *Shem ha-Gedolim,* ed. New York, n.d.

Baer, Y., "Religious Social Tendency of the Sefer Hasidim" (Hebrew) in *Zion,* vol. 3 (1938), pp. 1–50.

Bahya Ibn Pakudah, *Hovot ha-Levavot,* ed. P. J. Liebermann, Jerusalem, 1968.

Bakan, H. D., *Toledot Or ha-Hayyim ha-Kadosh,* New York, 1981.

Baruch of Kossov, *Amud ha-Avodah,* Tchernowitz, 1863.

Beer, M., "Regarding the Sources of the Number 36 Zaddikim" (Hebrew), in Churgin Memorial Volume, Bar-Ilan Annual, Jerusalem, 1963, pp. 172–175.

Ben-Amos, Dan, and Jerome R. Mintz, *In Praise of the Baal Shem Tov,* trans., Indiana University Press, Bloomington, 1970.

Ben-Sasson, H. H., "Kiddush ha-Shem and Hillul ha-Shem," in Encyclopedia Judaica, vol. 10, pp. 977–986.

Berger, Israel, *Eser Orot,* Warsaw, 1913.

Bilu, Yoram, "Dreams and the Wishes of the Saint," in *Judaism Viewed,* ed. Harvey E. Goldberg, Albany, 1987, pp. 285–313.

Bloch A. M., *Ruah Eliyahu,* 1988.

Blum, Mordecai, *U-Vo Tidbak,* Jerusalem, 1980.

Bornstein, Meir, *Imrey Tzaddikim,* Warsaw, 1896.

Brown, Francis, S. R. Driver, and C. A. Briggs, *Hebrew and English Lexicon of the Old Testament,* Clarendon Press, Oxford, 1906 (abbrev. BDB).

Brown, S. L., *The Book of Hosea,* Westminister Commentaries, London, 1932.

Buber, Martin, *For the Sake of Heaven,* Greenwood, New York, 1985.

Büchler, Adolf, *Types of Jewish Palestinian Piety from 70 B.C.E. to 70 C.E.: The Ancient Pious Men,* Oxford University Press, 1922.

Burrows, Millar, *An Outline of Biblical Theology,* Philadelphia, 1946.

Cohen, S., ed., *Peer ha-Dor,* 5 vols., Bene Berak, 1966–1973.

Cohn, Robert L., "Sainthood," in Encyclopedia of Religion, Macmillan, New York, 1987, vol. 13, pp. 1–6.

Cordovero, Moses, *Tomer Devorah,* ed. Z. W. Ashkenazi, Jerusalem, 1975; Eng. trans. L. Jacobs, "The Palm Tree of Deborah," London, 1960.

Cronbach, Abraham, "Social Thinking in the *Sefer Hasidim,*" in HUCA, vol. 22, 1949, pp. 1–147.

Dan, Joseph, *The Esoteric Theology of Ashkenazi Hasidism* (Hebrew), Jerusalem, 1968.

_____ *The Hasidic Story: Its History and Development* (Hebrew), Jerusalem, 1975.

_____ ed. *The Early Kabbalah,* New York, 1986.

Dov Baer, Maggid of Mesirech, *Or Torah,* Brooklyn, 1980.

Dressner, Samuel, H., *The Zaddik,* New York, n.d.

Dubnow, S., *Toledot ha-Hasidut,* Tel Aviv, 1967.

Dunner, N. N., *Mayyim Rabbim,* Warsaw, 1899.

Eleazar of Worms, *Sefer Rokeah ha-Gadol,* Jerusalem, 1967.

Elijah, Gaon of Vilna, *Commentary to Sifra de-Tzeniuta* (Hebrew), photocopy, Jerusalem, 1970.

Elimelech of Lizensk, *Noam Elimelekh,* ed. G. Nigal, Mosad Harav Kook, Jerusalem, 1978.

Elior, Rachel, "Between *Yesh* and *Ayin:* The Doctrine of the Zaddik in the Works of Jacob Isaac, the Seer of Lublin," in *Jewish History,* ed. Ada Rapoport-Albert, pp. 393–455.

Elleh Ezkerah, 7 vols., New York, 1956–1972.

Encyclopedia Talmudit, ed. S. J. Sevin.

Epstein, Joseph D., *Mitzvot ha-Bayit,* New York, 1975.

Etkes, Immanuel, "Rabbi Israel Salanter and his Psychology of Musar," in Green, *Jewish Spirituality,* vol. 2, pp. 206–244.

Feigenstock, A., *Toledot ha-Hatam Sofer,* New York, 1953.

Fine, Lawrence, *Safed Spirituality,* New York, 1984.

Frumkin, Michael, *Shivhey ha-Rav,* in *Sefarim Kedoshim,* vol. 27, New York, 1976.

Gershon Henoch of Radzhyn, *Sefer Orhot Hayyim,* Jerusalem, 1966.

Ginzberg, Louis, *Students, Scholars, and Saints,* New York, 1958.

Glenn, Menahem M., *Israel Salanter,* New York, 1953.

Goldberg, Harvey E., ed., *Judaism Viewed from Within and from Without,* State University of New York Press, Albany, 1987.

Goldberg, Hillel, *Israel Salanter,* Ktav, New York, 1982.

Goldziher, Ignaz, "Veneration of Saints in Islam," in his *Muslim Studies,* ed. S. M. Stern, vol. 2, London, 1971, pp. 255–341.

Green, Arthur, ed., *Jewish Spirituality,* Crossroad, New York, vol. 1, 1986; vol.

2, 1987, "Typologies of Leadership: The Hasidic Zaddik" pp. 127–156.

Greenstone, Julius H., *Proverbs,* Philadelphia, 1950.

Gries, Zeev, "The literature of hasidic rules (Hebrew)," in *Zion,* 46:3, pp. 198–235.

_____ "The sources and editing of the *Darkhey Tzedek.* Attributed to R. Zechariah Mendel of Yaraslov" (Hebrew), in *Jerusalem Studies in Jewish Thought,* vol. 2, Tishri-Kislev, Jerusalem, 1982, pp. 132–152.

_____ "The formation of the literature of Jewish rules at the end of the sixteenth and in the seventeenth centuries and its historical significance" (Hebrew), in *Tarbitz,* 56:4 (1987), pp. 527–581.

Gulkovitsch, Lazar, *Die Entwicklung des Begriffes Hasid im Alten Testament,* Tartu, 1934.

_____ *Die Bildung des Begriffes Hasid,* Tartu, 1935.

Günzig, J., *Die "Wundermänner" in jüdischen Volke,* Antwerp, 1922.

Guttmann, M. E., *Rabbi Dov mi-Leovo,* Tel Aviv, 1952.

Habermann, Jacob, *Maimonides and Aquinas,* Ktav, New York, 1979.

Hafetz Hayyim (Israel Meir Kagan), "The letters of the *Hafetz Hayyim*" in his *Collected Works,* New York, 1975.

Hayyim Haikel of Amdur, *Hayyim va-Hesed,* Jerusalem, 1970.

Hayyim of Volozhyn, *Nefesh ha-Hayyim,* Vilna, 1840.

Heilpern, Yehiel, *Seder ha-Dorot ha-Shalem,* Jerusalem, 1985.

Horowitz, Isaiah, *Sheney Luhot ha-Berit* (abbrev. *Shelah*), Jerusalem, 1963 and var. eds.

Husik, Isaac, *A History of Medieval Jewish Philosophy,* Meridian Books, New York, 1958.

Idel, Moshe, *The Mystical Experience in Abraham Abulafia,* trans. Jonathan Chipman, State University of New York Press, Albany, 1988.

Isaac of Acre, *Sefer Meirat Eynayim,* H. A. Erlanger, Jerusalem, 1975.

Israel of Koznitz, *Avodat Yisrael,* Lemberg, 1858.

Jacob Joseph of Pulnoyye, *Toledot Yaakov Yosef,* Warsaw, 1881.

_____ *Ben Porat Yosef,* Warsaw, 1883.

Jacob Zemah, *Shulhan Arukh ha-Ari,* var. eds., Munkacs, 1940.

_____ *Naggid u-Meztavveh,* Amsterdam, 1712.

Jacobs, Louis, "The concept of hasid in the biblical and rabbinic literature," in Journal of Jewish Studies, Oxford, vol. 8, nos. 3 and 4, 1957, pp. 143–154.

_____ *Seeker of Unity,* Vallentine, Mitchell, London, 1966.

_____ *Hasidic Prayer,* Routledge, London, 1972.

_____ *A Jewish Theology,* Darton, Longman and Todd, London, 1973.

_____ *Jewish Mystical Testimonies,* Schocken, New York, 1977.

_____ "How much of the Babylonian Talmud is pseudepigraphic?" in Journal of Jewish Studies, Oxford, vol. 28, no. 1, spring 1977, pp. 46–59.

James, William, *The Varieties of Religious Experience,* Longmans, Green, New York, 1905.

Jonah Gerondi, *Shaarey Teshuvah,* Vilna, 1896.

Judah he-Hasid, *Sefer Hasidim,* ed. J. Wistinetzki, Frankfurt-am-Main, 1924, and ed. Reuben Margaliot, Jerusalem, 1973.

_____ *Perushey ha-Torah,* ed. I. S. Lange, Jerusalem, 1975.

Kadish, Y. K., *Tiferet ha-Yehudi,* Pietrikow, 1913.

Kahana, David, *Bet Shlomo,* Orsheva, 1928.

Kaidenover, Jacob, *Sippurim Noraim,* Lemberg, 1875.

Kalisch, Zevi Elimelech, *Kevod Hakhamim,* Bene Berak, 1970.

Kaplan, Aryeh, *Rabbi Nahman's Wisdom,* New York, 1973.

Karo, Joseph, *Maggid Mesharim,* Amsterdam, 1704.

Katz, D., *Tenuat ha-Musar,* Zioni, Tel Aviv, 1958.

_____ *Pulmus ha-Musar,* Weiss, Jerusalem, 1972.

Klepholtz, Israel, *Sefer Torat ha-Maggid,* Tel Aviv, 1969.

_____ *Gedoley Hasidey Belz,* Bene Berak, 1974.

_____ *Sippurey Bet Din shel Maalah,* Bene Berak, 1978.

Lamm, Norman, *Torah Lishmah,* Mosad Harav Kook, Jerusalem, 1972.

Landau, B., *ha-Gaon he-Hasid mi-Vilna,* "Torah mi-Tzion," Jerusalem, 1978.

Langauer, E., *Tumat Kohanim be-Kivrey Tzaddikim,* in *Noam,* vol. 21, 1977, pp. 184–232.

Levi, A., *Od Yosef Hai* (Biography of Yosef Sholomo Dayyan), Jerusalem, 1986.

_____ *Derekh Tzaddikim,* Jerusalem, 1988.

Levi Yitzhak of Berditchev, *Kedushat Levi,* Jerusalem, 1964.

Lewin, B., ed., *Otzar ha-Geonim,* Gittin, Jerusalem, 1941.

Luzzatto, Moses H., *Mesillat Yesharim,* ed. M. M. Kaplan, Philadelphia, 1936.

Maimonides, Moses, *Mishneh Torah* (*Yad ha-Hazakah*) var. eds.

——— *Moreh Nevukhim,* Lemberg, 1866; English trans. *The Guide of the Perplexed,* by S. Pines, University of Chicago Press, 1974.

Malter, Henry, *The Treatise Ta'anit of the Babylonian Talmud,* Philadelphia, 1928.

Manasseh ben Yisrael, *Nishmat Hayyim,* Amsterdam, 1652.

Margaliot, Reuben, *Hilula de-Tzaddikaya,* Lemberg, 1929.

——— *Ner la-Maor,* Jerusalem, 1959.

Markus, Ivan G., "The Devotional Ideas of Ashkenazi Pietism," in Green, *Jewish Spirituality,* vol. 1, pp. 356–366.

Menahem Mendel of Premyslani, *Darkhey Yesharim,* Jerusalem, 1961.

Meshullam Phoebus of Zbarazh, *Yosher Divrey Emet,* in *Sefer Likkutim Yekarim,* Jerusalem, 1974, pp. 109–152.

Midrash Tanhuma, ed. M. Buber, photocopy, New York, 1946.

Mintz, Benjamin, *Sefer ha-Histalkut,* Tel Aviv, 1930.

Montefiore, C. G., and Herbert Loewe, *A Rabbinic Anthology,* London, 1938.

Mordecai of Tchernobil, *Likkutey Torah,* Lemberg, 1867.

Moses Hayyim Ephraim of Sudlikow, *Degel Mahaney Efrayim,* ed. Jerusalem, 1963.

Moskovitz, Zvi, *Otzar Sippurim* [in 20 parts], Jerusalem, 1951–1959, in *Sefarim Kedoshim,* vol. 28, New York, 1985.

——— *Maaseh Nehemiah,* Jerusalem, 1956.

——— *Berakhah Meshuleshet,* in *Sefarim Kedoshim,* vol. 17.

Nahman of Tcherin, *Lashon Hasidim,* Lemberg, 1876.

——— *Derekh Hasidim,* Lemberg, 1870.

Nahmanides, Moses, *Commentary to Pentateuch,* ed. H. D. Chavel, Jerusalem, 1960.

Nahshuni, Judah, *Rabbenu Moshe Sofer,* Mashavim, Jerusalem, 1981.

Oesterley, W. O. E., *The Jews and Judaism During the Greek Period,* London, 1941.

Otto, Rudolf, *The Idea of the Holy,* trans. G. W. Harvey, Oxford University Press, 1957.

Perl, Joseph, *Megalleh Temirin,* Vienna, 1819.

Pfeiffer, Robert H., *History of New Testament Times,* London, 1949.

Pietrikovsky, A., *Sefer Piskey Teshuvah,* Pietrikow, 1937.

Pinehas of Koretz, *Midrash Pinhas,* var. eds., in *Sefarim Kedoshim,* vol. 1, Brooklyn, 1979.

Plaut, Hezekiah, *Likkutey Haver Ben Hayyim,* vol. 3, Pressburg, 1880.

Poyetto, Jacob, *Kitzur Reshit Hokhmah,* Jerusalem, 1979.

Rabbinowitz, Y. M., *Afikey Yam,* Warsaw, 1935, Weingarten, Jerusalem, 1988.

Rafaeli, Y., *Ha-Rav Sharabi* (biography of Mordecai Sharabi), Jerusalem, 1985.

Rapoport-Albert, Ada, and Steven Zipperstein, eds., *Jewish History: Essays in Honour of Chimen Abramsky,* Weidenfeld, London, 1988.

Raza de-Uvda, on R. Eliezer Zeev of Kretchnef, Brooklyn, 1976.

Raziel, ed. Medzibezh, 1818.

Roth, Aaron, *Taharat ha-Kodesh,* Jerusalem, 1953, 3-vol. ed., Jerusalem, 1974.

Schatz Uffenheimer, Rivkah, *Quietistic Elements in Eighteenth-Century Hasidic Thought* (Hebrew), Magnes Press, Jerusalem, 1968.

Schechter, Solomon, *Studies in Judaism,* 3 vols., Philadelphia, 1908.

Scholem, Gershom G., *Major Trends in Jewish Mysticism,* 3rd ed., Thames and Hudson, London, 1955.

_____ *The Messianic Idea in Judaism and Other Essays,* Schocken, New York, 1971.

_____ *Sabbatai Sevi,* English trans., Routledge, London, 1973.

_____ Dibbuk (Dybbuk) in Encylopedia Judaica, vol. 6, pp. 19–20.

_____ *Kabbalah,* Keter, Jerusalem, 1974.

Schürer, E., *Geschichte des jüdischen Volkes im Zeitalter Jesu Christi,* Leipzig, 1909; new English ed., rev. and ed. Geza Vermes, Fergus Millar, and Matthew Black, Edinburgh, 1978.

Schwartz, A. J., *Derek ha-Nesher,* Galante, 1925.

Sevin, S., *Sippurey Hasidim,* Tel Aviv, 1957.

_____ *Ha-Modaim ba-Halakhah,* Jerusalem, 1980.

Sforno, Obadiah, *Commentary to Pentateuch,* in *Mikraot Gedolot,* Warsaw, 1860.

Shaarey Teshuvah (Geonic Responsa), ed. Y. Halevi, Leipzig, 1858.

Shapira, Hayyim Eleazar of Munkacs, *Divrey Torah,* Jerusalem, 1974.

Shneur Zalman of Liady, *Tanya,* Vilna, 1930.

_____ *Shulhan Arukh,* New York, 1976.

Shrock, A. T., *Rabbi Jonah ben Abraham of Gerona,* London, 1948.

Silver, Abba Hillel, *Where Judaism Differed,* New York, 1956.

Singer, Simeon, ed., *The Authorised Daily Prayer-Book,* London, 1962.

Sofer, Shlomo, *Hut ha-Meshulash,* Tel Aviv, 1963.

Soresky, Aaron, *Marbitzey Torah me-Olam ha-Hasidut,* Peer, Bene Berak, 1986–1987.

_____ *Be-Labbat Esh, Esh Dat,* Tel Aviv, 1985.

Tchernowitz, Chaim, *Pirkey Hayyim,* New York, 1954.

Teomim-Frankel, J. A., *Oholey Shem,* Bilgorej, 1911.

Tishby, Isaiah, "Zevi Hermann Shapira," in *Molad,* Jerusalem, 1972, p. 568.

Tractenberg, Joshua, *Jewish Magic and Superstition,* New York, 1970.

Tykochinsky, Y. M., *Gesher ha-Hayyim,* Jerusalem, 1960.

Tzavvaat ha-Ribash, Kehot, New York, 1975.

Urbach, E. E., *Hazal,* Jerusalem, 1969.

Urbach, S. B., *Amudey ha-Mahashavah ha-Yisraelit,* Jerusalem, 1954.

Uri of Strelisk, [teachings of] *Imrey Kodesh,* Jerusalem, 1961.

Uri Strelisker, *Petorta de-Abba,* Jerusalem, 1905.

_____ *Minhagey ha-Ari,* Jerusalem, 1975.

Van Der Leeuw, G., *Religion in Essence and Manifestation,* trans. J. E. Turner, London, 1938.

Vidas, Elijah de, *Reshit Hokhmah ha-Shalem,* ed. H. J. Waldmann, Jerusalem, 1980.

Vital, Hayyim, *Shaarey Kedushah,* Vilna/Grodno, 1834.

_____ *Sefer ha-Hezyonot,* ed. A. Eshkoli, Jerusalem, 1954.

Weintraub, J. D., *Sefer Tzavaot ve-Hanhagot,* Bene Berak, 1987.

Weiss, Joseph, *Studies in Eastern European Jewish Mysticism,* Oxford University Press, 1985.

_____ "The great maggid's theory of contemplative magic," in HUCA, vol. 31, 1960, pp. 137–147.

Weissberg, Joseph D., *Otzar ha-Hayyim Minhagey Tzanz,* Jerusalem, 1978.

Werner, D., *Tzaddik Yesod Olam,* Jerusalem, 1980.

Wertheim, A., *Halakhot ve-Halikhot ba-Hasidut,* Mosad Harav Kook, Jerusalem, 1960.

Wilensky, Mordecai, *Hasidim u-Mitnaggedim,* Mosad Bialik, Jerusalem, 1970.

Winkler, Gershon, *Dybbuk,* Judaica Press, New York, 1981.

Yehiel Michel of Zlotchow, *Mayyim Rabbinim,* ed. M. N. Kohen of Kolbiel, Warsaw, 1891.

Yehiel Moshe of Komararovka, *Sefer Niflaot Hadashot,* Pietrikow, 1897.

Yitzhak Eisik of Komarno, *Notzer Hesed,* Lemberg, 1862.

_____ *Hekhal ha-Berakhah,* Lemberg, 1869.

Zechariah Mendel of Yarolav, *Sefer Darkhey Tzedek,* Warsaw, 1877.

Zevi Elimelech of Dinov, *Derekh Pikkudekha,* ed. Jerusalem.

Zinberg, Israel, *A History of Jewish Literature,* trans. and ed. Bernard Martin, Cleveland, 1972.

INDEX